COLORADO
SCRAMBLES
Climbs Beyond the Beaten Path

THE COLORADO
MOUNTAIN CLUB
GUIDEBOOK

COLORADO
SCRAMBLES
Climbs Beyond the Beaten Path

SECOND EDITION

DAVE COOPER

The Colorado Mountain Club Press
Golden, Colorado

Colorado Scrambles: Climbs Beyond the Beaten Path
© 2009 Dave Cooper

PUBLISHED BY

 The Colorado Mountain Club Press
710 Tenth Street, #200, Golden, Colorado 80401
303-279-3080 ext. 2 I email: cmcpress@cmc.org

Founded in 1912, The Colorado Mountain Club is the largest outdoor recreation, education, and conservation organization in the Rocky Mountains. Look for our books at your local bookstore or outdoor retailer or online at www.cmc.org

CONTACTING THE PUBLISHER
We would appreciate it if readers would alert us to any errors or outdated information by contacting us at the address above.

Alan Bernhard—design and composition
Michelle Myers—proofreader
Dianne Nelson—copyeditor
Alan Stark—publisher

DISTRIBUTED TO THE BOOK TRADE BY
 Mountaineers Books
1001 SW Klickitat Way, Suite 201, Seattle, WA 98134, 800-553-4453,
www.mountaineersbooks.org

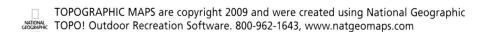 TOPOGRAPHIC MAPS are copyright 2009 and were created using National Geographic TOPO! Outdoor Recreation Software. 800-962-1643, www.natgeomaps.com

 We gratefully acknowledge the financial support of the people of Colorado through the Scientific and Cultural Facilities District of greater metropolitan Denver for our publishing activities.

COVER IMAGE: The author on the Northeast Ridge of Lone Cone. Photo by Charlie Winger.
FROSTISPIECE: Ginni Greer on Tijeras Peak.
IMAGE CREDITS: All images by the author, except as credited on individual photographs.

ISBN: 978-0-9799663-3-0
Printed in Korea

CONTENTS

COLORADO SCRAMBLES CHECKLIST

	DIFFICULTY	LENGTH	BACKPACK APPROACH	DATE COMPLETED
1. The Knife	2	3		
2. Lavender Peak & Mount Moss	2	2		
3. Arrow Peak	2	1	✔	
4. Trinity Traverse	2	2	✔	
5. Jagged Mountain	2	2	✔	
6. Pigeon Peak	2	2	✔	
7. Coxcomb	2	1	✔	
8. "Heisshorn"	2	1	✔	
9. "El Punto"	2	1	✔	
10. U.S. Grant	3	1	✔	
11. Pilot Knob	2	1	✔	
12. Vermillion and Golden Horn	1	1	✔	
13. Lookout Peak	1	1		
14. Southwest Ridge of Mt. Sneffels	1	2		
15. Engineer Mountain	1	1		
16. Lone Cone	3	1		
17. Milwaukee to Pico Asilado	2	3	✔	
18. Tijeras Peak	1	1	✔	
19. Music Mountain	3	2		
20. Crestone Traverse	3	3	✔	
21. Little Bear–Blanca Traverse	3	2	✔	
22. "Peak Q"	2	2	✔	
23. "Peak L"	2	1	✔	
24. "Peak R" & "Peak S"	2	2	✔	
25. Grand Traverse	3	3		
26. "West Partner Peak"	2	2		
27. "East Partner Peak"	2	2		
28. "Peak C"	2	2		
29. Gore Range Traverse	3	3		
30. Keller Mountain	1	2		
31. Tenmile Range Traverse	3	3		
32. Quandary Peak	3	2		
33. Pacific Peak	2	2		
34. Father Dyer Peak	1	1		
35. Mayflower Gulch Grand Traverse	3	3		
36. Ellingwood Ridge	3	3		
37. Ice Mountain	2	2		
38. Fools Peak	3	2		
39. S. Arapaho to N. Arapaho Traverse	2	2		
40. Mount Neva	2	2		
41. Lone Eagle Peak	3	1	✔	
42. Navajo Peak	2	2		
43. Little Pawnee to Pawnee Peak Traverse	2	2		
44. Mount Meeker and Longs Peak	2	3		
45. Little Matterhorn	2	2		
46. McHenrys Peak	2	2		
47. Mount Bierstadt to Mount Evans	1	2		
48. Torreys Peak	2	2		
49. The Citadel to Pettingell Traverse	2	2		
50. Mount Bancroft	2	1		

KEY   **DIFFICULTY:**   1 = Easy Scramble | 2 = More difficult | 3 = Hard
       LENGTH: 1 = A few hours | 2 = Moderate | 3 = A long day
       (does not include backpack approaches)

FOREWORD

Charlie Winger on Lone Cone.

If you had the foresight to purchase the first edition of Dave Cooper's *Colorado Scrambles: A Guide to 50 Select Climbs in Colorado's Mountains*, it's entirely possible that by this time it's dog-eared from (mis)use. Now, it's time to upgrade to the exciting new second edition, *Colorado Scrambles: Climbs Beyond the Beaten Path*. Here, you'll find new routes, updated route descriptions, and the outstanding photography you've come to expect from Dave's guidebooks. If *Beyond the Beaten Path* is your first Cooper book, then you're in for a rare treat. If you are lucky enough to have the out-of-print first edition of *Scrambles*, don't discard it; it's now a collector's item.

I've had the pleasure of hiking and climbing with Dave and his life partner, Ginni Greer, for nearly two decades. They seem to be getting older, but I'm just getting "more mature." The scrambles described in this guide bring back plenty of memories of the early days when we explored the mysteries of Colorado's mountains. As time passed, our ambitions and imaginations expanded to include climbing in areas around the world. Our adventures have included fun climbing trips in Bolivia, Peru, and Nepal, to name a few.

It's been said that "what comes around goes around," and now we find ourselves gradually returning to our roots and discovering that we don't need to travel worldwide to find mountaineering adventure; it's right here in our own backyard. Just take a look at the front cover if you don't believe that many Colorado climbs are *Beyond the Beaten Path*. Paths? We don't need no stinkin' paths!

So, lace up your boots and load up the pack—it's time to go experience those special climbs you've earmarked in this guide.

You're obviously interested in purchasing this guidebook, so why not also pick up a copy of the mega-classic, *Colorado Snow Climbs: A Guide for All Seasons*, also by Dr. Cooper. One cannot own too many guidebooks. Trust me.

CHARLIE WINGER
Somewhere beyond the beaten path
March 2008

ACKNOWLEDGMENTS

A guidebook is usually the result of many peoples' efforts. This book is no exception. Without the help and hard work of many friends, this book would not exist.

First, thanks are due to Terry Root and Charlie Winger for encouraging me to take on this project. Their help and support have been invaluable.

Many people have provided input for the selection of routes presented in this guide. Their huge combined experience has enabled the guide to encompass not only the well-known classics but also little-known gems. Some of these people are Jean Aschenbrenner, Trace Baker, Dan Bereck, Gary Hoover, Debby Reed, Terry Root, and Charlie Winger. I thank any people not mentioned here for the informal discussions of routes that have helped make this a better guide.

A special thanks to the people who climbed these routes with me—the shared experience is, for me, what makes mountaineering special. These include Gary Hoover, Charlie and Diane Winger, Randy Murphy, Gerry Roach, Debby Reed, Ginni Greer, Dwight Sunwall, Dan Bereck, Dan Blake, Dan Stright, Gary Neben, Diana and Kevin Craig, Laura Zaruba, Mike Keegan, John Jennings, and members of Colorado Mountain Club trips who accompanied me on several of these routes. Also, thanks to Tyler Griffith and partner, who provided enjoyable companionship when we joined up on the Ellingwood Ridge on La Plata Peak. The loss of Vern Lunsford, my climbing partner for many years while we explored Colorado's mountains, to an avalanche in 2003 has left a large gap. I missed not having his companionship while climbing many of these routes. I believe he was with me in spirit.

Perhaps the most important characteristic of a climbing guide is accuracy. I thank Beth Schlicter, Ward Hobert, Doug Kruesi, Bill Tarvin, Terry Root, and Linda Grey for field-checking several of the routes and providing additional photographs. Charlie Winger, Ginni Greer, and Dan Bereck have spent countless hours reviewing draft manuscripts.

Additional excellent photographs have been provided by Gary Hoover, Charlie and Diane Winger, Dan Bereck, and Ginni Greer. A special thanks goes to Ryan Schilling for his great photographs and route recollections of the Trinity Traverse.

I would like to thank National Geographic for granting permission to use their Topo!® software. It has added tremendous clarity to the route descriptions.

Engineer Mountain.

Woody Smith, keeper of the Colorado Mountain Club Archives, provided invaluable assistance in researching the climbing history of the routes and mountains contained in this guide. The wonderful book *Roof of the Rockies* by William H. Bueler is one of my favorites, providing a tremendously interesting historical perspective on the exploration of Colorado's mountains. The exploits of Colorado's early mountaineers humble us all.

In my wanderings in Colorado's mountains, a number of guidebooks have been of great assistance. The ones that especially come to mind are: Gerry Roach's guides covering the Indian Peaks, Rocky Mountain National Park, and the Fourteeners; Garratt and Martin's groundbreaking guide to *Colorado's High Thirteeners*; Robert F. Rosebrough's *Climbing Colorado's San Juan Mountains*; Robert Ormes's *Guide to the Colorado Mountains*; Richard Rossiter's *Rocky Mountain National Park—The High Peaks*; and Joe Kramarsic's book on the Gore Range, *Mountaineering in the Gore Range: A Record of Explorations, Climbs, Routes and Names*. A book can only be as good as the editing. My thanks to copyeditor Dianne Nelson and publisher Alan Stark for keeping me on track, and Alan Bernhard for the outstanding layout design.

Finally, I want to thank Ginni for putting up with my long absences and obsessive behavior during the researching and writing of this book. Thanks for your patience, Ginni, as well as for all of your help. I couldn't have done it without you.

—DAVE COOPER

PREFACE

A few years ago, I found myself nearing completion of my peak lists for Colorado's highest mountains. The Fourteeners and Centennial lists converged at about the same time. The list of bicentennial peaks was also well under way. However, while the lists provided a peak-climbing agenda, I found that I wasn't looking forward to attacking more lists of peaks; some were sure to be challenging, but many were simple walkups. I felt that I needed a fresh challenge to keep my interest level high. In the meantime, friends and I had made a number of trips to the South American Andes and Alaska, plus a few forays onto other great mountains within the continental United States.

I found myself spending more time rock and ice climbing and less time hiking up Colorado's high peaks. In fact, I was using them more to prepare for expeditions than to climb them for their own sake. As my friends and I started to attempt more difficult routes elsewhere, the need for more appropriate and challenging training climbs in Colorado became evident.

We started to seek out third-, fourth-, and fifth-class routes on Colorado's peaks. We were also climbing snow and alpine ice routes, plus winter peaks, but that left much of the summer climbing season open for other challenges. The fifth-class routes were challenging and fun, but the ability to move lighter, and therefore faster, on third- and fourth-class terrain made these "scrambling" routes fun and addicting. We looked for ridge runs, enchainments of multiple peaks, and challenging routes on familiar peaks that perhaps had "easier" normal routes.

As we pursued our goal to become well-rounded mountaineers for "foreign" climbs, we found that the "training" climbs we were uncovering in Colorado were just as fun and satisfying as the climbs for which we were training.

This book attempts to share the fun and excitement that we have found on scrambling routes in Colorado.

Some routes included here are well-known classics; however, I have added less-well-known routes of equal quality. Peak elevation has not been a factor in choosing routes for this guide; there are high-quality routes to be found on twelve- and thirteen-thousand-foot peaks as well as on the Fourteeners. Many climbers have provided input and suggestions for routes worthy of inclusion. I sincerely appreciate all of this input. It makes this a better guide by exposing us to some of the favorite routes of climbers with a huge combined experience in the Colorado mountains.

Ask twenty climbers for their list of the fifty best scrambles, and you are sure to come up with twenty different lists. As you look at the list presented here, you may ask, "Why didn't he include the X ridge on Y peak?" The truth is that the list could include a hundred, two hundred, or more great scrambling routes. Nevertheless, I hope that as you explore the routes described here, you will agree that these represent the wonderful diversity of climbs in our state.

I have attempted to include scrambles of varying difficulty and commitment. These can provide a progression for climbers just starting to explore the world of more difficult high peak routes. The description presented in the **OVERVIEW** of each route, in conjunction with the Scrambles Checklist (see page 7) information ranking the commitment of the climbs, should allow you to select routes appropriate to your experience and skill level.

If you don't have the skills necessary to attempt a particular climb, get instruction and/or find partners who are willing to train you safely in these skills. People have died or been seriously injured on many of these routes.

Even experienced scramblers can get themselves into trouble on routes included here. The objective dangers on these routes are significantly greater than those encountered at your local crag, where risks are normally managed by the use of ropes and rock protection. One of the reasons we climb is to challenge ourselves in order to discover more about ourselves; therefore, we must be willing to accept responsibility for our actions and decisions. How else can we grow as climbers (and perhaps in other ways too)?

Climbing is an activity to be undertaken with friends. While it was necessary to solo a number of the routes in this book in order to document the routes (you can't always find partners who can climb seven days a week), I find that being able to share the experience with good friends is what climbing is about. It is also much safer in the event of a problem. Experience tells us that not all of our decisions are correct. Being able to discuss route options with a climbing partner makes for a safer outing.

I have attempted to provide enough route details to enable you to follow the classic lines you are trying to find, without detracting from the challenge of route finding that is intrinsic to scrambling. I hope I have achieved the right balance. This is not meant to be a how-to guide!

INTRODUCTION

WHAT IS SCRAMBLING?

Scrambling encompasses the realm between off-trail hiking and technical climbing. Routes described here involve substantial amounts of second-, third-, and fourth-class climbing (see the section on **Climbing Grades** [page 15] for definitions of climbing difficulty).

Scrambling is the efficient movement over challenging and often exposed terrain without the need to rope up (although ropes will be needed for short sections on some of these routes).

Rarely will you find these routes completely clear of snow. In fact, snow travel is an integral part of scrambling in Colorado. Snow can make a route easier or more difficult. Good early-season conditions can offer excellent moderate and steep snow climbing, often without needing ropes and protection. (I will also argue that unless you are traveling on crevassed terrain—rare in Colorado—roped climbing dictates the use of some form of protection, at least at belay stances. Simulclimbing without placing intermediate protection rarely makes sense.)

ABOUT THIS GUIDE

This guide is written for the experienced climber. ***People have died on these routes.*** While the element of risk is always there, even for the experienced, skill and judgment can make a huge difference in your chance of becoming a statistic.

Remember that the most critical item in your climbing arsenal is your brain. Good judgment, good route-finding abilities, and experience will do more to keep you out of trouble than the best piece of equipment in your pack. If you don't have the experience to tackle these routes, there are many excellent schools willing to teach you. I gained many of the skills necessary to climb routes like these through The Colorado Mountain Club. I recommend investigating what the club has to offer.

There is no substitute for getting out there and gaining experience on easier routes. You will be exposed to the vagaries of Colorado's weather and learn to make route decisions and go/no-go decisions based on a variety of factors, including the strength of the group, equipment malfunctions, time of day, weather, difficulty of terrain, and route conditions (snow, wet rock, and ice, for example). Go with friends whose judgment you trust. Better to learn by observing good judgment than by having epics.

This guide should get you to the start of a route and give you sufficient information to complete the route. Having said that, the guide does not provide blow-by-blow details of every step along a route. As mentioned earlier, a part of the challenge and enjoyment of scrambling is in the route finding.

I hope that the extensive use of photographs to show crux spots will help you decide whether to climb an obstacle directly or skirt around it. Even so, I guarantee that on occasion you'll still have to backtrack a bit to find a reasonable downclimb. That's the nature of scrambling! An open mind and a sense of adventure are requirements.

USING THIS GUIDE

Scrambles described in this guide are arranged by mountain range, in no specific order. Some of the larger ranges are further divided into sub-ranges.

Each sub-range has an introductory section that provides general information about the area and about the rock to be found there. While I am definitely no geologist, I find myself critically interested in the quality of the rock I will encounter on a climb.

The introduction to an area provides overview maps and, in some cases where several routes are contained within a relatively small area, the route map as well.

For all routes described in this guide, critical information is highlighted at the beginning of each section. **ROUND-TRIP DISTANCE**, **ROUND-TRIP TIME** for an "average experienced scrambler,, **STARTING ELEVATION** and **HIGHEST ELEVATION** are provided, as well as **ELEVATION GAIN**. **SEASON** indicates the months when a scramble is likely to be in good condition. **JURISDICTION** and **MAPS** (which refers to USGS maps) information is provided. The **OVERVIEW** of each scramble briefly describes the highlights and difficulty of the route. Detailed information for each scramble is provided in the **GETTING THERE**, **APPROACH**, and **ROUTE DESCRIPTION** sections.

A couple of comments here on statistics: You may find that you climb a route more slowly than the guide says, or possibly faster. I've tried to be consistent in the time estimates, so after doing a couple of these routes, you should be calibrated.

I have made no effort to give a time estimate for the backpacking approaches. People tend to backpack at very different speeds. Because all backpacks in this book are on established trails (with the possible exception of the Vestal Creek Trail and the Ruby Creek approach), you should be able to estimate the time required for an approach based on the elevation gain and distance and on your own past experiences.

The **COMMENT** section of each scramble provides a little background that may be of interest.

The **ROUTE DESCRIPTION** is meant to be used with the route map and GPS waypoint information. Photographs should also be helpful in route finding and should provide a "feeling" for the difficulty and quality of the route. Some photographs have a red route line superimposed, typically on the more complex routes.

Maps and GPS Waypoints

The maps show both approach and scrambling routes. These routes have, in almost every case, been collected in the field using Global Positioning System (GPS) receivers. Although generally excellent, a few factors can reduce accuracy. Most tracks were collected using a Magellan SportTrac Pro®. I have found this receiver to have better reception than most devices when the sky is obscured by trees. However, there are still times when a loss of accuracy seems to occur. Other situations that can cause loss of accuracy are in narrow gullies and in climbing situations when the climber's body tends to block the signals.

Sometimes on an approach, the track deviates from a trail shown on the USGS maps. I tend to believe the GPS data in these cases. Usually this is not a cause for concern, since trails shown on the USGS maps tend to be well-defined. Just stay on the trail.

GPS waypoints are provided for critical points on a route. These should be used in conjunction with a good map. And don't forget to ensure that the datum on your GPS receiver is matched to the map. All GPS data in this guide uses NAD83 for the datum.

Remember that having a GPS receiver doesn't mean that you shouldn't still have (and be competent in using) a map and compass.

Climbing Grades

Mountaineering: The Freedom of the Hills (6th Edition, The Mountaineers Books) describes the following classes for rock climbing, based on the Yosemite Decimal System.

CLASS 2: Simple scrambling, with possible occasional use of the hands.

CLASS 3: Scrambling; a rope might be carried.

CLASS 4: Simple climbing, often with exposure. A rope is often used. A fall on Class 4 rock could be fatal. Typically, natural protection can be easily found.

CLASS 5: Where rock climbing begins in earnest. Climbing involves the use of a rope, belaying, and protection (natural or artificial) to protect the leader from a long fall.

A few of the climbs in this book involve Class 5 climbing under good conditions. All of the climbs in this guide involve Class 3 and/or Class 4 scrambling and, of course, much Class 2 terrain.

Grading routes is somewhat subjective. Regional variations abound. There is as much discussion about grades as about climbing ethics, the weather, or any other items of interest to mountaineers. This guide attempts to use consistent ratings based on the consensus opinion of many experienced mountaineers in Colorado.

As Robert Rosebrough says in his excellent guidebook *Climbing Colorado's San Juan Mountains*, "Class 4 is one of the most subjective ratings." One working definition might be that, irrespective of whether or not members of a group use a rope to climb up Class 4 terrain, they will likely want the security of a rope when descending the same terrain.

An example of a Class 4 pitch is the summit pitch on Crestone Needle, when doing the Crestone Traverse. Experienced climbers with a technical (Class 5) background often climb this pitch without a rope, while other climbers with whom I've talked—experienced scramblers—would be terrified to climb this without the protection of a rope. Almost everyone, however, will rappel the pitch if descending.

In this guide, the terms Class 3, Class 4, and Class 5 are used interchangeably with third class, fourth class, and fifth class.

Commitment grades are based on the National Climbing Classification System (NCCS).

GRADE I: Normally requires several hours; can be of any technical difficulty.

GRADE II: Requires half a day; any technical difficulty.

GRADE III: The climbing requires a day.

GRADE IV AND ABOVE: In addition to longer, more committing climbs, these grades indicate successively more technical content.

No routes in this guide are harder than Grade III, while most are either Grade I or Grade II. Note that approaches (including backpacks) are not generally included when grading a route.

Equipment and Clothing

It is assumed that the user of this guide is familiar with the basics of clothing and gear needed for mountaineering in Colorado. The trick is to carry everything you may need, but no more.

As I get older and smarter (feebler?), I pay more attention to the weight on my back and feet.

Certainly you need to carry the ten essentials, but it is possible to minimize the weight of these items.

A backpack that can carry everything to base camp, then be stripped down for the climb, is a big plus. For the last few years I've been using one pack for just about everything: the Arc'teryx NoZone.® This is my ice-climbing pack, Colorado backpack, summit pack, and expedition pack on climbs such as Ama Dablam, Aconcagua's Polish Glacier, and climbs in the Alaska Range. It carries weight well, climbs well with its optional waistband, and strips down to be lightweight. The volume can be supplemented with side pockets when needed. For a medium-size pack like this to work, it obviously takes some effort to refine your clothing and gear needs.

Occasionally, on routes with many pitches of alpine rock, or on long enchainments, I will use a Camelbak®-style pack.

Weight on your back makes a huge difference when moving fast on third- and fourth-class terrain. The weight on your feet is also a factor. Certainly, for early-season scrambles where snow and ice can be encountered (not to mention muddy trails), a good, moderately stiff-soled leather mountaineering boot is appropriate. I like one that takes a step-in crampon in addition to being stiff enough to kick steps.

During mid- to late-summer conditions, one of the great variety of "approach shoes" can make scrambling much more fun. The light weight and sticky rubber soles are perfect for something like the Ellingwood Ridge on La Plata or the Little Bear–Blanca Traverse.

As far as equipment goes, your choice depends on the route and conditions. Early-season climbs may dictate the use of crampons and an ice ax, especially for those early-morning starts.

We carry a rope on many of these routes—often just a 75-foot, 9-millimeter rope. A rope provides insurance in the event the rock is iced up or wet, or if (heaven forbid) we get off route. Also, if your party needs to self-evacuate after an accident, a rope becomes a necessity. An example of a route where a short 75-foot rope is adequate (and likely to be used) would be the Citadel to Pettingell Traverse.

On routes that we know ahead of time will require a long rappel, we will take an appropriately long 9-millimeter rope (usually 50 meters long). Bring along some kind of lightweight harness for these situations. Examples of routes like this would be Coxcomb and Bancroft.

Very few of these scrambles require a technical climbing rack. If needed, a small mountaineering rack consisting of 5 to 6 stoppers and 4 to 5 cams up to a number 3 Friend®, and a few standard runners with carabiners, should be adequate. An example of a route where a small rack might be used is for the North Ridge on Quandary Peak.

If we are carrying a rope, we always also bring a couple of 10-foot, neutral-colored slings to use for anchors. **Make sure that you know how to rig a rappel or belay anchor safely.** Rappels are one of the main sources of climbing accidents, usually because of anchor failure. Get qualified instruction on how to build anchors.

Pickets may be of use on some of the snow climbs. The gully leading to the Moss–Lavender Col may require a picket or two when climbed on snow.

OBJECTIVE HAZARDS

These are real hazards that you should be able to evaluate before and during a climb. Remember that there are usually no absolute answers to the question, "How safe are the _____ conditions today?" Play it safe and err on the side of caution.

Although we all hope that accidents won't occur, be prepared to deal with such an eventuality. Obtain training in mountain-oriented first aid and carry a first aid kit. Become familiar with self-rescue techniques. Rescue by an organized rescue group may be many hours away.

While cell phones may be useful in an emergency, don't become dependent on them. Remember that in many areas of our mountains there is no coverage.

Weather

During the summer months, the main concern is often about thunderstorms, but remember that they can also occur during other times of the year. You can be chased off a ridge in May by thunderstorms while being snowed on.

An early season snowstorm that moved in as we were starting our descent.

Several people are killed or injured every year in Colorado by lightning strikes. Plan to be off summits and ridges by noon in the summer. Be prepared to bail if the weather threatens. Identify escape routes ahead of time. The mountain will be there the next time. Make sure that you will be!

During one of my first Fourteener climbs (Wetterhorn), we were surprised by a morning thunderstorm while on the very exposed summit (we had no warning before the lightning hit; no distant peals of thunder). We descended rapidly, glissading snowfields (a good reason to carry an ice ax) for a couple of thousand feet before we felt safe. Imagine our surprise when we ran into some hikers still climbing up, even though they had seen our near miss. Use common sense.

The weather in Colorado's high country can change very rapidly, catching scramblers unaware. Snowstorms can occur during any month of the year.

Avalanches

I've often heard it said that "there are no experts when it comes to predicting avalanches." While I believe this to be largely true, understanding how to interpret snow stability can at least allow you to make informed decisions concerning route choices. Winter and spring are, of course, the seasons when this is likely to be an issue.

Take an avalanche awareness course, know the history of the snowpack, and check current conditions (http://avalanche.state.co.us/index.php).

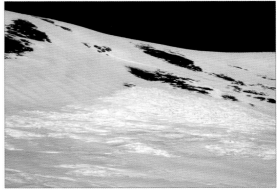

A recent slide covered the trail on the approach to the Torreys-Kelso ridge.

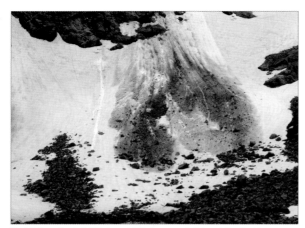

Rockfall on Peak Q. We heard this large rockslide while climbing an adjacent peak. The rock came down a possible route that we might have taken the next day.

Rockfall

This is most likely to occur in the spring due to freeze-thaw cycling or when the ground becomes saturated due to snowmelt, or after heavy rains during the summer months. It is hard to predict. Watch for rockfall in gullies. If conditions are suspect, traveling through the danger zone may be best before the sun hits the rock, while things are still frozen.

Rockfall can be spontaneous or triggered by climbers. Try not to climb above or below other groups, and either negotiate a loose gully one at a time or keep your group close together. Wear helmets! Learn to move carefully on loose talus and scree, being careful not to dislodge rocks.

Exposure and Rock Conditions

Climb within your limits and be able to protect yourself and other members of your party on exposed terrain. Remember that poor rock quality or snow/ice may make a section of a climb much more serious. Learn to test handholds and footholds and how to weight them safely. Sometimes a loose handhold can be used by pulling or mantling straight down, while an outward pull would dislodge it. Similarly, a foothold can sometimes be stabilized by stepping on it in such a way that your weight pushes it into the ground.

SUMMARY

Scrambling can be a rewarding way to discover the wild places of Colorado (and perhaps learn more about yourself). I hope you get as much joy and satisfaction from these routes as I and my friends have.

BACKCOUNTRY ETHICS

The outings in this guide traverse a number of publicly managed land units, including wilderness areas, national parks, and national forests. Remember, also, that private land often abuts these units. Respect any private property and "no trespassing" postings. Additionally, federal law protects cultural and historic sites on public lands such as old cabins, mines, and Native American sites. These historic cultural assets are important to all of us as a society and should not be scavenged for personal gain.

U.S. Forest Service occupancy regulations are primarily designed to limit wear and tear in fragile wilderness areas. However, even non-wilderness areas need to be treated lightly to preserve resources for future generations. Strive to leave no trace of your passing, and follow the principles of Leave No Trace (LNT).

The LNT message promotes and inspires responsible outdoor recreation through education, research, and partnerships. Managed as a nonprofit educational organization and authorized by the U.S. Forest Service, LNT is about enjoying places like the Colorado Rockies while traveling and camping with care.

Before starting your outing, check with the U.S. Forest Service for the current forest fire danger, which can sometimes be extreme, and for any restrictions on campfires. Jurisdiction for each of the scrambles will be found at the beginning of each description.

Leave No Trace

The seven LNT principles of outdoor ethics form the framework of LNT's message:

1. Plan ahead and prepare
2. Travel and camp on durable surfaces
3. Dispose of waste properly
4. Leave what you find
5. Minimize campfire impacts
6. Respect wildlife
7. Be considerate of other visitors

LEAVE NO TRACE, INC.
P.O. Box 997
Boulder, CO 80306
(800) 332-4100
(303) 442-8217 Fax
www.lnt.org

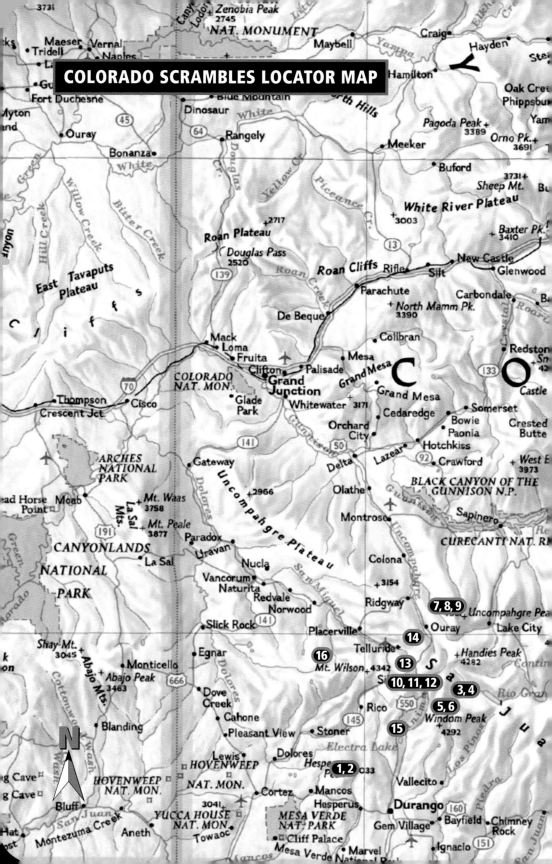

COLORADO SCRAMBLES LOCATOR MAP

COLORADO

Range · Coalmont · Gould · Clark Peak +3947 · Fort Collins · Laporte · Ault · Briggsdale · New Raymer

Masonville · Windsor · Eaton · Galeton

ROCKY MT. · Estes Park +4133 · Loveland · Greeley · Gill · Kersey · Riverside Res. · Jackson · Weld

Rabbit Ears Pass 2873 · Parkview Mt. +3748 · NAT. · Berthoud · Lyons · Johnstown · Milliken · La Salle · Gilcrest · Platteville · Orchard

Grand Lake · **44, 45, 46** · Longmont · Platteville · Fort Lupton · Roggen · Keenesburg · Wiggins · 52

+3257 · 40 · ARAPAHO NAT. RECREATION AREA · L. Granby · Frederick · Erie · Lafayette · Hudson · Empire Res.

Kremmling · **41** · Granby · Boulder · Louisville · Brighton

Hot Sulphur Springs · Tabernash · Fraser · **39, 40, 42, 43** · Northglenn · Thornton

Bond · Winter Park · Berthoud Pass · Moffat Tunnel · Westminster · Arvada · Denver · Watkins · Bennett · Strasburg · Byers

29 · 3449 · **50** · Central City · Golden · Lakewood · Aurora

25, 26, 27, 28 · **22, 23, 24** · **49** · Idaho Springs · **Denver** · Deer

Eagle · **30** · 3655 · **48** · Loveland Pass · Evergreen · Englewood · Littleton

Minturn · Frisco · Dillon · **47** · Bow Mar · Indian Hills · Conifer · Parker

38 · Red Cliff · **31** · Grays Pk. · Mt. Evans +4346 · Bailey · Louviers · Sedalia

34, 35 · Breckenridge · Shawnee · Buffalo Creek · Castle Rock · Kiowa · Elizabeth

Climax · **32, 33** · Alma · 285 · Larkspur · 86 · Elbert

Tennessee Pass · 3177 · Bison Peak +3789 · Cheesman L. · Palmer Lake · Simla · Ramah

36 · Mt. Elbert +4399 (14433 ft) · Twin Lakes · Leadville · Fairplay · Hartsel · Lake George · Woodland Park · Monument · U.S. AIR FORCE ACADEMY · Black Forest · Calhan

37 · Mt. Harvard +4395 · Elevenmile Canyon Res. · Florissant · Cascade · Pikes Peak +4301 · Manitou Springs · Ellicott · Yoder · Rush

Buena Vista · Currant Creek Pass · FLORISSANT FOSSIL BEDS NAT. MON. · Security · Colorado Springs · Horse

Nathrop · 2896 · Cripple Creek · Victor · Widefield · Fountain · FORT CARSON

Pitkin · Ohio · +4349 · Maysville · Salida · Cripple Creek · Royal Gorge · Broadmoor

Monarch Pass · 3448 · Poncha Sprs. · Lincoln Park · Canon City · Penrose · Portland · North Avondale · Boone · Crowley

Sargents · Mt. Ouray +4258 · Rockvale · Florence · Coal Creek · Avondale · Fowler · Oln

114 · Coaldale · Cotopaxi · Wetmore · **Pueblo** · Rocky F

3093 North Pass · Villa Grove · Westcliffe · Silver Cliff · Beulah · St. Charles · Manzanola

Cochetopa Hills · Saguache · 9 · Colorado City · Rye · 10

Luis Peak 3307 · Storm King Mt. · Moffat · +4292 Challenger Point · Greenhorn Mt. +3764 · 1963 · 1964 · Rattlesnake Buttes

GREAT SAND DUNES NAT. MON. · **17, 18, 19, 20** · Gardner · Walsenburg

Center · Hooper · Red Wing · North La Veta Pass 2869 · Apishapa

Del Norte · Mosca · Pryor · Model

Monte Vista · Blanca Peak +4372 · **21** · 160 · La Veta · +3866 · Aguilar · Model Reservoir

Wolf Creek Pass 3309 · Homelake · Alamosa · Blanca · Cuchara · +3866 Spanish Peaks · Hoehne

Summitville · Summit Pk. +4054 · Platoro · La Jara · Sanford · San Acacio · San Luis · Stonewall · Jansen · Cokedale · Trinidad · +Fishers Peak 2934

Romeo · Conejos · Manassa · San Pablo · Chama · Weston · Segundo · Starkville

17 · Antonito · La Vall

La Plata Range

From left to right, Hesperus, Lavender, and Moss dominate this view of the La Plata Range.

PHOTO BY DAN BERECK

This seldom-visited range contains some spectacular scenery and fine scrambling. Located northwest of Durango, this compact range is dominated by Hesperus Mountain (13,232 feet).

The main access routes into the range are from the town of Mancos on the range's southwest side (for the Sharkstooth Trailhead) and from the town of Hesperus north along La Plata Canyon (for the Knife Trailhead). The latter area is heavily used, and you will find camping restrictions in place. There are, however, several designated camping areas along the canyon.

The access roads are generally good, graded dirt; however, the four-wheel-drive roads up Boren Creek and Tomahawk Basin are very rough. On one climbing trip in this area, I managed to destroy two tires simultaneously. Luckily, some passing ATV riders stopped and kindly provided a plug kit to allow temporary repairs. A friend also had a small, electric compressor to re-inflate the tires. These items are now a part of my emergency kit.

The area has been mined extensively. An interesting exhibit a few hundred feet up the Sharkstooth Pass Trail (on a spur trail loop) is worth visiting. Information displays explain some of the mining history.

The mountains and connecting ridges of the La Platas offer solitude, challenging scrambles, and beautiful scenery. During the course of several forays into this area, I have never encountered other climbers, except on the walkup routes on Hesperus Mountain and Centennial Peak.

The prominent rock banding on Hesperus Mountain.
PHOTO BY DAN BERECK

THE ROCK

The striking "banded" appearance of Hesperus Mountain and some of its neighbors is due to the intrusion of igneous rock (or sills) into the shales of the area. The sills form the lighter-colored rock between the brown shales.

1. The Knife—
Babcock Peak to Spiller Peak

The Knife, seen from Hesperus, showing the multiple summits of Babcock Peak at left and Spiller Peak at right.

ROUND-TRIP DISTANCE	2.2 miles from the mine; 7.6 miles from the trailhead
ROUND-TRIP TIME	5 hours from the mine
STARTING ELEVATION	11,197 feet at the mine; 9,260 feet at the trailhead
HIGHEST ELEVATION	13,149 feet
ELEVATION GAIN	2,200 feet from the mine; 4,200 feet from the trailhead
SEASON	Late June to October
JURISDICTION	San Juan National Forest, Columbine, and Mancos/Dolores Ranger Districts
MAP	La Plata 7.5 minute

OVERVIEW: A hike or drive up a four-wheel-drive road, a scramble up gullies to two summits (Class 3), followed by a long ridge traverse (Class 3). A long descent down scree and talus.

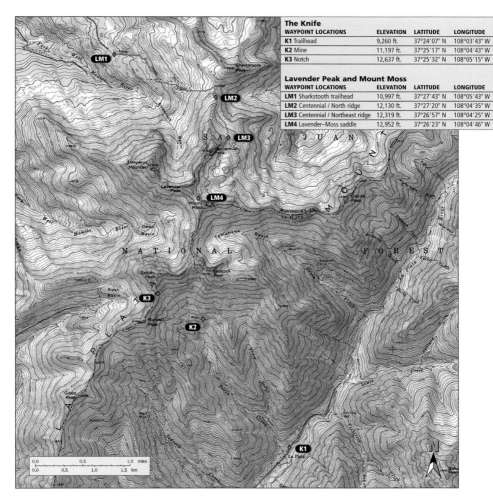

The Knife			
WAYPOINT LOCATIONS	**ELEVATION**	**LATITUDE**	**LONGITUDE**
K1 Trailhead	9,260 ft.	37°24'07" N	108°03'43" W
K2 Mine	11,197 ft.	37°25'17" N	108°04'43" W
K3 Notch	12,637 ft.	37°25'32" N	108°05'15" W

Lavender Peak and Mount Moss			
WAYPOINT LOCATIONS	**ELEVATION**	**LATITUDE**	**LONGITUDE**
LM1 Sharkstooth trailhead	10,997 ft.	37°27'43" N	108°05'43" W
LM2 Centennial / North ridge	12,130 ft.	37°27'20" N	108°04'35" W
LM3 Centennial / Northeast ridge	12,319 ft.	37°26'57" N	108°04'25" W
LM4 Lavender–Moss saddle	12,952 ft.	37°26'23" N	108°04'46" W

GETTING THERE: From the west end of the small town of Hesperus on U.S. 160, drive north for 8.5 miles on the La Plata Road to its junction with Boren Creek Road by the La Plata Townsite. From the trailhead at this junction (K1), hike or drive 2.7 miles and 2,000 feet up the four-wheel-drive road to the old mine at 11,197 feet (K2).

COMMENT: Babcock Peak to Spiller Peak via the Knife is one of the finest ridge traverses in the state. The Knife looks fearsome from any vantage point, but in reality this ridge is quite moderate, although you can expect significant exposure in places.

   The ridge is not the place to be in a thunderstorm, since there are essentially no bailout spots once you commit to it.

The ridge actually runs from the west summit of Babcock over to Spiller, but the middle summit of Babcock is the high point. (The quad shows the east summit as the high point, but this is another error on this quad, leading some people to refer to this quad as the "lemon quad"). The route described climbs both the middle and west summits of Babcock.

The most common approach for Babcock is from Tomahawk Basin. However, for the Knife it makes more sense to use the access provided by the Boren Creek Road (also, as mentioned elsewhere, I have an aversion to the Tomahawk Basin approach).

ROUTE DESCRIPTION: From the vicinity of the mine at 11,197 feet, head uphill on initially grassy slopes that become talus. Aim for the farthest left of three gullies, and enter this at 12,400 feet.

Note that the gully, even though it is south-facing, can hold snow well into July. Head up the gully until it starts a turn to the left. Look for an obvious narrow, loose gully

Approaching the three gullies from the mine. The left gully provides access to Middle and West Babcock Peaks.

taking off to the right at this point. This gully provides access to the south ridge of Middle Babcock. To climb the middle summit, head up this narrow gully, and upon reaching the ridge, scramble up on good Class 3 terrain to the summit.

It is possible, though not recommended, to rappel from the middle summit to the top of the notch between the middle and west summits. Solid anchors are hard to find, and there is considerable danger of the rope bring-

ing down rocks as you rappel. It is better to reverse your route to the gully and continue up to the notch.

From the notch it is a simple scramble to the top of the west summit.

From here, take a look at the ridge over to Spiller Peak. This is the infamous Knife. It takes about an hour to scramble across the ridge to the obvious notch just before Spiller, but

Starting the traverse across the Knife.   PHOTO BY DAN BERECK

An exposed section near the end of the traverse.

Climbing the gully to Spiller's summit.   PHOTO BY DAN BERECK

it can take almost another hour to negotiate the notch and climb to the summit of Spiller; make sure that the weather will cooperate. There are few (if any) opportunities to escape the ridge.

The ridge is beautiful, with excellent scrambling on reasonably good rock (be sure to test holds, though).

In general, it is possible (and best) to stay right on the ridge. Never descend more than a few feet. Some sections have amazing exposure, but the scrambling arguably does not exceed Class 3.

After reaching the major notch in the ridge, descend into it on the right side of the ridge. Downclimb the north couloir below the notch for 150 feet until you can gain grassy ledges in a shallow gully on the west side of the notch, toward Spiller. This gully provides fun third- class scrambling all the way to the summit of Spiller and avoids a second notch in the ridge.

Descend the ridge connecting to Burwell Peak on a loose, gravelly trail. When you reach a notch (K3), head down tedious, steep scree and angle back toward the mine (K2).

Looking down the ridge from Spiller to Burwell.

2. Lavender Peak and Mount Moss

Lavender and Moss, seen from Hesperus. Moss is at the far right.

ROUND-TRIP DISTANCE	6.4 miles (4 miles on trail)
ROUND-TRIP TIME	8 hours
STARTING ELEVATION	10,997 feet
HIGHEST ELEVATION	13,192 feet
ELEVATION GAIN	2,700 feet
SEASON	Late June to October
JURISDICTION	San Juan National Forest, Columbine, and Mancos/Dolores Ranger Districts
MAP	La Plata 7.5 minute

OVERVIEW: A good approach on trails with a moderate scramble to Moss and a more challenging scramble to the summit of Lavender. Reaching the saddle between Moss and Lavender may require very steep snow climbing until well into the season.

SEE MAP PAGE 27

GETTING THERE: From the town of Mancos on U.S. 160 (approximately 20 miles west of Durango), turn north on Colorado 184. After 0.3 mile, turn right on Forest Service Road 561 (aka County Road 42) at the sign for Transfer Campground and the Sharkstooth Trailhead. Reach Transfer Campground at the 10-mile point. Stay on Forest Service Road 561 for 2 more miles, following the signs, until half a mile past the Aspen Ranger Station. Take a right turn onto Forest Service Road 350 (again, well signed). After 4 miles, the road forks again, the left fork being Forest Service Road 351 and the right fork Forest Service Road 350. Stay right; 2.5 miles further the road forks again. Take the right fork, signed to the Sharkstooth Trailhead, which you will reach in 1.5 miles. This last mile and a half may be a little rough for some passenger cars.

COMMENT: The elevations of these peaks are in dispute by many climbers. The consensus seems to be that Lavender is higher than Moss. It certainly looks to be.

The snow-filled gully in the center of this photo leads to the Lavender-Moss saddle.

Climbing the snow gully to the Lavender-Moss saddle.

PHOTO BY DAN BERECK

The route described starts at the Sharkstooth Trailhead. This is not the normal approach to these peaks, but the excellent access to this trailhead (which is also the starting point for Hesperus Mountain—13,232 feet), perhaps combined with some reluctance on my part to drive into Tomahawk Basin, makes this approach quite attractive.

Lavender Peak in particular is remarkably rugged, especially its ridges over to adjoining Centennial Peak and Hesperus. These ridges are quite serious and are not recommended due to the very loose rock combined with the technical rating on the Centennial ridge. The ridge joining Lavender to Moss is much more reasonable, although you still have to deal with some challenging scrambling to reach Lavender's exposed summit.

ROUTE DESCRIPTION: From the Sharkstooth Trailhead (LM1), follow the excellent trail 2 miles to Sharkstooth Pass. Turn right and start up the broad north ridge on Centennial. At 12,130 feet (LM2), drop off the ridge and contour below the mass of Centennial to cross the northeast ridge at LM3. From here you have a good view of the route up to the Lavender-Moss saddle (LM4). The gully up to the saddle holds snow for a long time. The photos on pages 31 and 32 were taken on July 11.

Head for the base of the narrow gully below the saddle.

The snow-filled gully can be quite a demanding climb. When we climbed this, the snow had drifted in to form a 20-foot section of 60- to 70-degree slope. You may want to protect this.

The gully is about 2 pitches in length, with a good belay/rappel point two-thirds of the way up in the rocks on your left. On reaching the saddle, Moss is a straightforward scramble to your left.

For Lavender, return to the saddle and head up the ridge, reaching a

The step used to gain access to the gully between west (left) and east (right) summits is directly above the climber's head.   PHOTO BY DAN BERECK

minor ridge point just before the twin peaks of the summit. Downclimb into a small gully, cross it, and climb up a step on the lower east summit. This will put you in a good position to climb up the gully separating the two summits.

Scramble up the final gully, and again head left to the west summit and convince yourself that it is the higher of the two. The east summit may also be reached from the saddle.

The summit block isn't difficult to climb on its back side, but it is small. You don't want to stand up on it in a high wind.

The final gully leading to the notch between Lavender's summits.

Grenadier Range

The sweeping east faces of the Grenadier Range.

No one who has ever made the long backpacking approach will doubt that this is one of the least-accessible ranges in Colorado. It is also one of the most rewarding climbing areas with unique geologic features creating stunning landscapes.

This range offers many long, technical climbs on excellent rock, including Wham Ridge on Vestal Peak. The Center Route on Wham Ridge (5.6 to 5.7) is a personal favorite.

Also of excellent quality are many scrambling routes, two of which are described here.

In this section, in addition to the written description, a map has been included for the approach to Arrow Peak and the Trinity Traverse. Access to this area is normally from Elk Park via the Elk Creek and Vestal Creek drainages. How you get to Elk Park depends on your preference. You can take the narrow-gauge railroad from Durango (described in the Needles Section) or hike in from Molas Pass.

History
The second ascent of Arrow was made on August 11, 1932 by Carleton Long and John Nelson from Arrow Lake, on the south side of the peak.

The characteristic faulting and uplifting can be seen in this photo of Vestal Peak, taken from the summit of Arrow Peak.

THE ROCK

The striking east faces of the Grenadiers, as well as the relatively solid climbing to be had, are a result of the quartzite in the area, one of the hardest rocks in Colorado. The faulting and uplifting can be seen along the whole range.

Their difficult ascent line, via the Graystone–Arrow saddle, was not recommended for future climbers. (This ascent, believed by Long and Nelson to be the first of Arrow Peak, was recorded in *Trail and Timberline*, Number 169, November 1932. In fact, the peak had been climbed previously by William Cooper [no relation] and John Hubbard on July 15, 1908, the same day they made the first ascent of Vestal Peak [William H. Bueler, *Roof of the Rockies*, p. 169]).

According to *Roof of the Rockies*, the first ascent of the West and Middle Trinities was made during the 1941 Colorado Mountain Club outing when Schnackenberg, Burrows, Patterson, and Stewart made the first traverse of the Trinities by the route described in this guidebook.

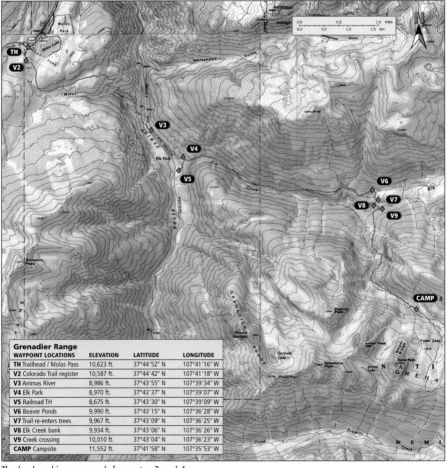

Grenadier Range			
WAYPOINT LOCATIONS	**ELEVATION**	**LATITUDE**	**LONGITUDE**
TH Trailhead / Molas Pass	10,623 ft.	37°44'52" N	107°41'16" W
V2 Colorado Trail register	10,587 ft.	37°44'42" N	107°41'18" W
V3 Animas River	8,986 ft.	37°43'55" N	107°39'34" W
V4 Elk Park	8,970 ft.	37°43'37" N	107°39'07" W
V5 Railroad TH	8,675 ft.	37°43'30" N	107°39'09" W
V6 Beaver Ponds	9,990 ft.	37°43'15" N	107°36'28" W
V7 Trail re-enters trees	9,967 ft.	37°43'09" N	107°36'25" W
V8 Elk Creek bank	9,934 ft.	37°43'06" N	107°36'26" W
V9 Creek crossing	10,010 ft.	37°43'04" N	107°36'23" W
CAMP Campsite	11,552 ft.	37°41'58" N	107°35'53" W

The backpacking approach for routes 3 and 4.

3. Arrow Peak—Northeast Face

A view of Arrow Peak on the approach.

ROUND-TRIP DISTANCE	18 miles backpacking from the Molas Pass Trailhead or 10.2 miles backpacking from Elk Park; 2 miles scrambling from meadow camp
ROUND-TRIP TIME	3.5 hours from camp
STARTING ELEVATION	11,400 feet
HIGHEST ELEVATION	13,803 feet
ELEVATION GAIN	Backpacking: 3,050 feet plus 2,140 feet to be re-climbed on the way out if starting at Molas Pass or 3,050 feet from Elk Park; 2,230 feet scrambling from camp
SEASON	July to September
JURISDICTION	San Juan National Forest, Columbine Ranger District, Weminuche Wilderness
MAP	Storm King Peak 7.5 minute

OVERVIEW: A long backpack to a camp below Vestal Lake and a short steep scramble on Class 3 and possibly Class 4 terrain.

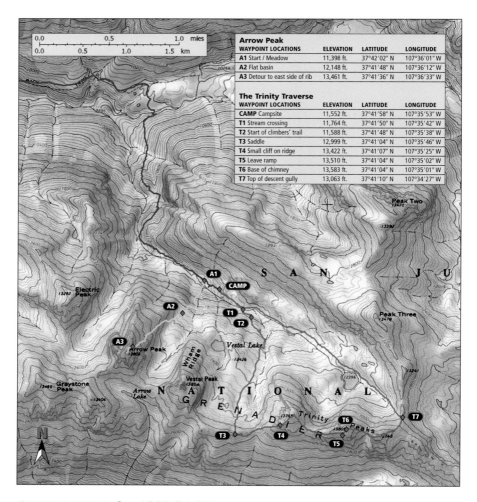

Arrow Peak			
WAYPOINT LOCATIONS	**ELEVATION**	**LATITUDE**	**LONGITUDE**
A1 Start / Meadow	11,398 ft.	37°42'02" N	107°36'01" W
A2 Flat basin	12,148 ft.	37°41'48" N	107°36'12" W
A3 Detour to east side of rib	13,461 ft.	37°41'36" N	107°36'33" W

The Trinity Traverse			
WAYPOINT LOCATIONS	**ELEVATION**	**LATITUDE**	**LONGITUDE**
CAMP Campsite	11,552 ft.	37°41'58" N	107°35'53" W
T1 Stream crossing	11,764 ft.	37°41'50" N	107°35'42" W
T2 Start of climbers' trail	11,588 ft.	37°41'48" N	107°35'38" W
T3 Saddle	12,999 ft.	37°41'04" N	107°35'46" W
T4 Small cliff on ridge	13,422 ft.	37°41'07" N	107°35'25" W
T5 Leave ramp	13,510 ft.	37°41'04" N	107°35'02" W
T6 Base of chimney	13,583 ft.	37°41'04" N	107°35'01" W
T7 Top of descent gully	13,063 ft.	37°41'10" N	107°34'27" W

GETTING THERE: See APPROACH

COMMENT: Many people consider this to be the finest scramble in the area. Sustained frictioning on steep quartzite and a stunning location make it a must-do route.

APPROACH: If you take the train from Durango, exit the train at Elk Park. Walk east for 100 yards to the start of the Elk Creek Trail (V5). [Map page 36]

Follow the Elk Creek Trail north up the hill for a short distance to where it meets the Colorado Trail at waypoint V4.

If you elect to hike in from Molas Pass, drive to the trailhead, 1.1 miles north of the pass and 5.4 miles south of Silverton on U.S. 550 (the Million

Dollar Highway).
Trailhead parking is
on the east side of
the highway, a short
distance off the road.
The road to the
parking area is
signed to Molas Lake
and the Molas Trail.

The route uses the two prominent ramps on Arrow's Northeast face.

Cross to the south
side of the parking
area where the trail
takes off (TH). After
200 yards, the trail
becomes the Colo-
rado Trail, marked by an information board and sign-in register (V2). The
excellent trail drops 1,700 feet to the Animas River in 3.3 miles, something
to look forward to on the way out.

Cross the substantial bridge across the Animas River and walk 0.1 mile
southeast along the railroad tracks to waypoint V3, where the trail leaves
the tracks and heads up the hill to join the trail coming up from the Elk
Park stop (V4). V3 is at the southeast end of a beaver pond.

From V4, the route is now the same, no matter how you got to this point.
Follow the Colorado Trail as it heads into the Weminuche Wilderness, and
go up Elk Creek for 2.8 miles from V4 to large beaver ponds at V6. The
unmaintained trail up Vestal Creek takes off from the far east end of the
ponds. The view of Arrow and Vestal from here is hard to ignore.

Follow the faint trail south, past the ponds and into a clearing with a
few campsites. The trail re-enters the trees at V7 and drops sharply down
the banks of Elk Creek at V8. Find a spot to cross the creek (this will vary
by time of year, but in late summer, a good spot can be found where two
large trees span the creek). Cross to the south side of the creek and regain
the trail at V9. The trail up Vestal Creek isn't too difficult to follow from
here, but downed timber makes it a bit challenging to stay on it the whole
way. In general, the trail stays well above the creek on its east side until
11,000 feet, where you follow the creek as it turns southeast and climbs
into the lower meadow at 11,400 feet. If you are lucky, you may be treated
to a spectacular sunset on Vestal and the Trinities.

Scrambling up to the summit,   PHOTO BY CHARLIE WINGER
just below the north ridge.

Camping spots away from the stream are scarce. A good place to camp is at waypoint CAMP, above the meadow. This puts you in good position for the Trinities, although you will have to backtrack down into the meadow for the takeoff for Arrow.

ROUTE DESCRIPTION: From the meadow at 11,400 feet (A1), take the climbers' trail southwest to the relatively flat basin between Arrow and Vestal peaks (A2) at about 12,150 feet. The route can be seen in its entirety from this spot.

A faint climbers' trail will help get you started. Head up to a grassy area, just out of view to lower right in the photo on page 39, and work your way onto the large, sweeping ramp. Continue up the ramp, either frictioning up the ramp proper or on more moderate terrain on its left (east) side. As the angle becomes steeper, the ramp divides into two levels. Work your way onto the upper (right-hand) level, and continue up its east (left-hand) margin as it narrows into a rib of rock.

As this rib becomes steeper, it may be necessary to make a short diversion onto its left (east) side (A3), but immediately regain the top of the rib.

The ramp narrows and steepens as you near the low point of the north ridge. Just before reaching the ridge, look for a cairned route on your left (east) that leads to the summit, or choose a slightly more difficult route closer to the ridge.

To descend, carefully retrace your steps.

This route is not the place to be during a rainstorm. The quartzite slabs, so much fun when dry, can become your worst nightmare when wet.

4. The Trinity Traverse

The three peaks of the Trinity Traverse.

ROUND-TRIP DISTANCE	18 miles backpacking from the Molas Pass Trailhead or 10.2 miles backpacking from Elk Park; 4.8 miles scrambling (from meadow camp)
ROUND-TRIP TIME	6 to 7 hours from camp
STARTING ELEVATION	11,552 feet at camp
HIGHEST ELEVATION	13,805 feet
ELEVATION GAIN	Backpacking: 3,050 feet plus 2,140 feet to be re-climbed on the way out if starting at Molas Pass, or 3,050 feet from Elk Park; 3,350 feet scrambling from a camp in the Vestal Creek drainage (CAMP)
SEASON	July to September
JURISDICTION	San Juan National Forest, Columbine Ranger District, Weminuche Wilderness
MAP	Storm King Peak 7.5 minute

OVERVIEW: A long backpack to a camp below Vestal Lake, with a long, challenging scramble over three summits.

SEE MAP PAGE 38

GETTING THERE: See APPROACH.

COMMENT: In his *Guide to the Colorado Mountains*, Robert Ormes refers to this traverse as "one of the finest scrambling traverses in the San Juans."

In the heart of the Grenadier Range, flanked by stunning peaks such as Arrow, Vestal, and Storm King, and providing unparalleled views of the Needle Mountains, this traverse would be worthwhile just for its surroundings. Add to that challenging scrambling and route finding and it has to be a must for your "to-do" list.

APPROACH: If you take the train from Durango, exit the train at Elk Park. Walk east for 100 yards to the start of the Elk Creek Trail (V5). [Map page 36]

Follow the Elk Creek Trail north up the hill for a short distance to where it meets the Colorado Trail at waypoint V4.

If you elect to hike in from Molas Pass, drive to the trailhead, 1.1 miles north of the pass and 5.4 miles south of Silverton on U.S. 550 (the Million

A view of Middle Trinity Peak and beyond from the West summit.

Dollar Highway). Trailhead parking is on the east side of the highway, a short distance off the road. The road to the parking area is signed to Molas Lake and the Molas Trail.

Cross to the south side of the parking area where the trail takes off (TH). After 200 yards, the trail becomes the Colorado Trail, marked by an information board and sign-in register (V2). The excellent trail drops 1,700 feet to the Animas River in 3.3 miles, something to look forward to on the way out.

Cross the substantial bridge across the Animas River and walk 0.1 mile southeast along the railroad

Climbers on the ledge leading from the saddle between West and Middle peaks to a point below the summit of Middle Trinity. This ledge provides access to the Class 4 chimney, the key to gaining the middle summit.   PHOTO BY RYAN SCHILLING

tracks to waypoint V3, where the trail leaves the tracks and heads up the hill to join the trail coming up from the Elk Park stop (V4). V3 is at the southeast end of a beaver pond.

From V4, the route is now the same, no matter how you got to this point. Follow the Colorado Trail as it heads into the Weminuche Wilderness, and go up Elk Creek for 2.8 miles from V4 to large beaver ponds at V6. The unmaintained trail up Vestal Creek takes off from the far east end of the ponds. The view of Arrow and Vestal from here is hard to ignore.

Follow the faint trail south, past the ponds and into a clearing with a few campsites. The trail re-enters the trees at V7 and drops sharply down the banks of Elk Creek at V8. Find a spot to cross the creek (this will vary by time of year, but in late summer, a good spot can be found where two large trees span the creek). Cross to the south side of the creek and regain the trail at V9. The trail up Vestal Creek isn't too difficult to follow from here, but downed timber makes it a bit challenging to stay on it the whole

The Class 4 chimney, key to ascending Middle Trinity.

way. In general, the trail stays well above the creek on its east side until 11,000 feet, where you follow the creek as it turns southeast and climbs into the lower meadow at 11,400 feet. If you are lucky, you may be treated to a spectacular sunset on Vestal and the Trinities.

Camping spots away from the stream are scarce. A good place to camp is at waypoint CAMP, above the meadow. This puts you in good position for the Trinities, although you will have to backtrack down into the meadow for the takeoff for Arrow.

ROUTE DESCRIPTION: From the meadow at 11,400 feet, follow the Vestal Creek Trail southeast, then cross to the stream's south side at T1. Almost immediately, find a climbers' trail (T2) that starts to make an ascending

Looking back at the east ridge of Middle Trinity Peak. The gully used for the descent from the summit can be seen just south (to the left in this photo) of the ridge.

traverse southeast up the hillside and continues into the high meadow between Vestal and West Trinity. The trail dies out in this meadow, so just head toward the saddle (T3).

The climbers' trail re-emerges in the loose gully below the saddle. From this saddle, the trail contours to the base of the west ridge of West Trinity, slightly south of the ridge, which you can climb either on or slightly south of the ridgeline, following cairns (Class 3). At waypoint T4, a small cliff will force you to the ridge crest. Follow the ridge the rest of the way to the summit (2 hours from camp).

From the top of West Trinity, the route over to Middle Trinity is quite impressive, with the knife-edge section quite visible. Expect to spend 1.5 hours on this segment.

East Trinity from Middle Trinity, showing the ascent gully south (right) of the ridge.

Easily descend the east ridge to the saddle between West and Middle peaks. From here, follow a cairned traverse on a significant ledge on the south side of the ridge that stays well below the knife-edge, a prominent feature just before the summit block of Middle Trinity.

The trick is not going too far on the ledge system. As it traverses a series of rock ribs, keep an eye peeled for cairns leading up an ascending traverse (T5), which you follow for 300 feet until you are stopped by a Class 4 chimney (T6), the crux of the route. Climb the chimney for 30 feet, exit and continue moving right, following the cairned route on an ascending traverse using ledges interspersed with short upclimbs to the summit of Middle Trinity.

Descend a loose gully south of the ridge to the saddle between Middle and East Trinities, seen in the photo on page 45.

Cross below the saddle and climb the gully south of the west ridge of East Trinity. I found the rock to be more enjoyable on the left side of this gully.

The gully reaches the south ridge of East Trinity a short distance below the summit. Follow this south ridge to the summit. Expect to spend a little more than an hour on the traverse from the Middle to East peaks. Continue down the straightforward north ridge of East Trinity on plates of slate to a notch at waypoint T7.

From this notch, drop into the basin at the head of the Vestal drainage. Stay north of the unnamed lake at 12,396 feet, and continue along the north side of the stream, eventually picking up the faint Vestal Creek Trail that you follow back to camp.

Note that there is a faint cairned trail that runs all the way up the drainage to the low point on the East Trinity–Peak 3 saddle. This provides an alternate but longer descent route from East Trinity.

Descending the north ridge of East Trinity Peak.   PHOTO BY RYAN SCHILLING

Needle Mountains

The Needles, seen from West Trinity.

Possibly the most rugged area of the state, the Needles are also the most remote. Composed largely of granite, they have resisted weathering to become the largest concentration of fourteen- and high thirteen-thousand-foot peaks Colorado has to offer.

Usually accessed from the Durango & Silverton Narrow Gauge Railroad, this area is heavily used by people climbing the Chicago Basin Fourteeners. Other parts of the range remain quite pristine. This section of the guidebook describes forays into two of these areas for scrambles on two of the most significant peaks in the area.

Although other approaches may be used, the most common way to access Jagged and Pigeon peaks is by train.

For information on the Durango & Silverton Narrow Gauge Railroad, call 970-247-2733 or go to www.durangotrain.com.

Both approaches start at the Needleton Trailhead. The backpacking approaches for Jagged and Pigeon are described under their respective

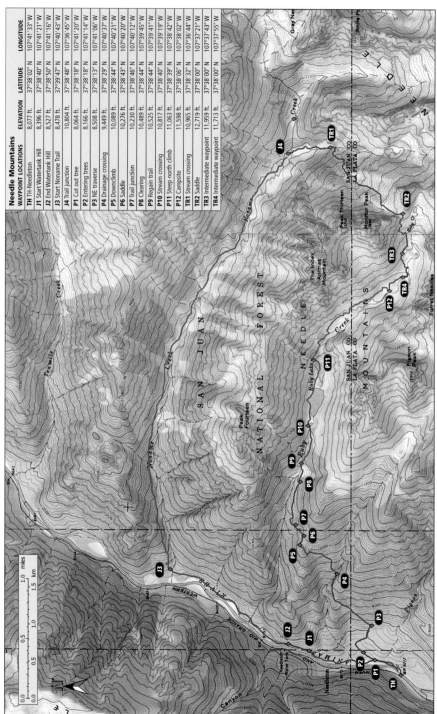

Needle Mountains WAYPOINT LOCATIONS	ELEVATION	LATITUDE	LONGITUDE
TH TH-Needleton	8,077 ft.	37°38'02" N	107°41'33" W
J1 Start Watertank Hill	8,396 ft.	37°38'40" N	107°41'21" W
J2 End Watertank Hill	8,527 ft.	37°38'50" N	107°41'16" W
J3 Start Noname Trail	8,478 ft.	37°39'47" N	107°40'43" W
J4 Trail junction	10,804 ft.	37°38'48" N	107°36'45" W
P1 Cut cut tree	8,064 ft.	37°38'18" N	107°41'20" W
P2 Entering trees	8,166 ft.	37°38'18" N	107°41'14" W
P3 NE traverse	8,508 ft.	37°38'13" N	107°41'06" W
P4 Drainage crossing	9,449 ft.	37°38'29" N	107°40'37" W
P5 Downclimb	10,089 ft.	37°38'44" N	107°40'21" W
P6 Saddle	10,276 ft.	37°38'43" N	107°40'20" W
P7 Trail junction	10,230 ft.	37°38'46" N	107°40'12" W
P8 Clearing	10,489 ft.	37°38'44" N	107°39'45" W
P9 Regain trail	10,525 ft.	37°38'44" N	107°39'41" W
P10 Stream crossing	10,817 ft.	37°38'40" N	107°39'19" W
P11 Steep north climb	11,063 ft.	37°38'39" N	107°38'42" W
P12 Campsite	11,598 ft.	37°38'06" N	107°38'02" W
TR1 Stream crossing	10,965 ft.	37°38'32" N	107°36'44" W
TR2 Saddle	12,719 ft.	37°38'00" N	107°37'21" W
TR3 Intermediate waypoint	11,959 ft.	37°38'00" N	107°37'43" W
TR4 Intermediate waypoint	11,713 ft.	37°38'00" N	107°37'55" W

The backpacking approaches for routes 5 and 6. Also shown is the route connecting the Noname and Ruby Creek drainages.

sections, starting at the Needleton Trailhead. Since many climbers are interested in combining scrambles in both the Noname and Ruby Creek drainages, the traverse between them is described here. We have run into several parties that have bushwhacked their way between the drainages without realizing that there is a perfectly serviceable, little-used trail. In sections, it is difficult to follow, but it is definitely worth the effort.

Connecting the Noname and Ruby Creek Drainages

From the camp in the Noname drainage, follow the trail south, continuing past the Jagged turnoff, as if heading up the unnamed drainage ending below the Twin Thumbs. The trail stays on the east side of the stream until TR1, where it crosses to the west side. Shortly after crossing the stream, the obvious trail heads up a steep hillside north of a small drainage. The trail becomes less distinct as it climbs toward tree line below the impressive east face of Monitor Peak.

After reaching tree line, head for the pass between Monitor and an unnamed point at 12,719 feet (TR2). The trail descends into Ruby Creek, hugging the right side of the drainage (under Monitor Peak), before dropping down to the valley floor shortly after TR3. The trail is difficult to follow in the area between TR2 and TR3, where it skirts to the right of a small rock outcrop. A possible camping area may be found just below this outcrop, at P12.

The Durango & Silverton Narrow Gauge Railroad.

History

Pigeon Peak was first ascended in 1908 by William Cooper and John Hubbard (on the same trip during which they made first ascents of Vestal and Arrow). For more information on this amazing duo and their climbing adventures, read William H. Bueler's *Roof of the Rockies*.

Jagged Peak was first ascended by a strong group of climbers from the San Juan Mountaineers during August 1933. As reported in *Trail and Timberline* (Number 181, November 1933), this group, consisting of Carleton Long, Dwight Lavender, T. Melvin Griffith, Lewis Giesecke, and H.L. McClintock, ascended the peak from the south side. Due to the technical nature of this route, subsequent climbs have been made from the north via the route described in this guide.

THE ROCK

The striking vertical relief of the Needles is courtesy of the granite of which most of these peaks are composed. As it decomposes, the granite is also responsible for the gravelly ledges that can make scrambles more challenging.

5. Jagged Mountain

Jagged and Gray Needle from Noname camp.

ROUND-TRIP DISTANCE	14 miles backpacking; 5 miles scrambling
ROUND-TRIP TIME	8 to 10 hours from camp
STARTING ELEVATION	8,077 feet at Needleton; 10,804 feet at J4 camp
HIGHEST ELEVATION	13,824 feet
ELEVATION GAIN	3,000 feet backpacking; 3,300 feet scrambling
SEASON	Late June to September
JURISDICTION	San Juan National Forest, Columbine Ranger District, Weminuche Wilderness
MAPS	Storm King Peak 7.5 minute; Snowdon Peak 7.5 minute

OVERVIEW: A long backpack into the heart of the Needle Mountains, with a difficult scramble requiring a rope (at least for the descent) and complex route finding.

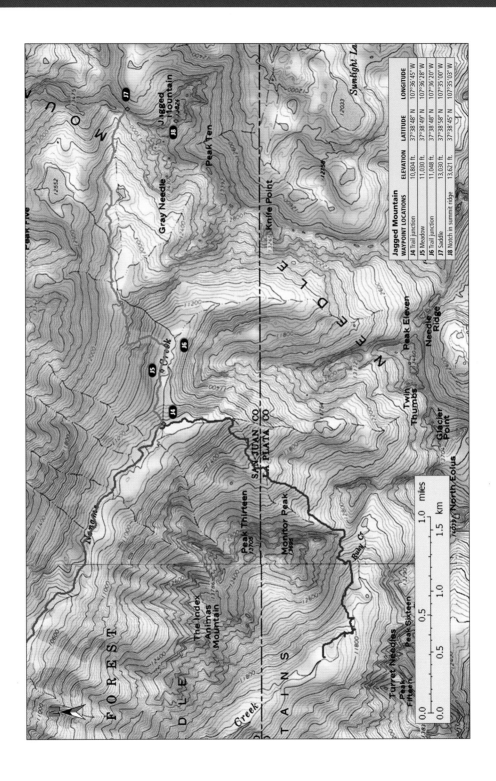

Jagged Mountain			
WAYPOINT LOCATIONS	ELEVATION	LATITUDE	LONGITUDE
J4 Trail junction	10,804 ft.	37°38'48" N	107°36'45" W
J5 Meadow	11,030 ft.	37°38'49" N	107°36'28" W
J6 Trail junction	11,048 ft.	37°38'48" N	107°36'20" W
J7 Saddle	13,030 ft.	37°38'58" N	107°35'00" W
J8 Notch in summit ridge	13,621 ft.	37°38'45" N	107°35'03" W

The north face of Jagged from the Jagged-Leviathan saddle. The route ascends gravelly ledges and rock steps immediately right of the snow-filled gully.

GETTING THERE: Take the narrow-gauge railway from Silverton or Durango to Needleton (TH).

COMMENT: A book of Colorado scrambles *must* include this one. With interesting scrambling, great views, and a remote location, Jagged has it all.

The first time I climbed this peak, with Dan Bereck, we combined it with Pigeon in a three-day blitz from the Needleton Trailhead. Utilizing the "light and fast" approach, we were down to one energy bar between us by the time we caught the train out. That's not the normal combination of climbs in this amazing area, but it remains a memorable trip.

APPROACH: The normal approach to Jagged Mountain uses the Noname Creek route described here. [See map on page 49.]

From Needleton (TH), cross the Animas River via the conveniently located footbridge and hike north along the sometimes hard-to-follow trail on the east bank of the river, crossing Pigeon Creek, North Pigeon Creek, and Ruby Creek along the way.

Climbing the ledge system to the right of the snow-filled gully.

After 0.9 mile (J1), the flat trail becomes a nasty scramble to bypass a cliff band (Watertank Hill) on steep, slippery, social trails for a few hundred yards until you're past this obstacle (J2). Continue on the flat trail and cross to the north side of Noname Creek after 2.4 miles. Locate the Noname Creek Trail 0.1 mile beyond the creek (J3). Look for a trail leaving the Animas River Trail at this point and heading right, up the hill. The remains of an antique telephone pole will be seen shortly after starting up the hill. This makes a good landmark. The trail, which is well cairned, leads directly to the Noname Creek Trail. This is an excellent trail, but if you aren't able to find it, you won't be going anywhere. Some faint trails head up the hillside directly after crossing the creek. They should eventually meet the Noname Trail, but be aware that the trail starts out quite high on the north side of the drainage. The trail stays on the north side of the creek the whole way, sometimes being quite high above the creek.

After a total distance of 7 miles backpacking, you will find good camping in a large meadow at about 10,770 feet, shortly after passing an old cabin, just before the trail divides at J4. It is possible to continue another 0.35 mile to a second opening (J5) or even higher, but the lower campsites

View of the southwest face of Jagged. The traverse ledge is shown in red.

are within striking distance of Jagged and are close to the limit of a reasonable day's backpacking approach.

ROUTE DESCRIPTION: From the camp at 10,770 feet, follow Noname Creek to the east end of the meadow (J4), where the trail starts to climb steeply through the trees to the east. Enter a higher meadow at J5 and continue to a trail junction at J6. Take the left branch (the right branch would take you up to the basin below Knifepoint and Sunlight Peak). Continue on to a basin above tree line at 11,800 feet. Here you can see the saddle north of Jagged at the east end of this basin. Climb to this saddle at 13,030 feet (J7) on a rough trail that stays north of the marshy area in the center of the basin and climbs steeply through some cliff bands before engaging the usual loose talus and scree slopes below the saddle. This is the pass between the Noname and Sunlight drainages.

From this saddle, you have a good view of the north face of Jagged (see photo on page 54). The route traverses into the bowl below this face at the 13,000-foot level on a faint trail (stay above the lower slabs) to a point just to the right of a deep couloir splitting the face (this couloir often has snow in it).

The normal route starts in a wet chimney just down and left of an alternate start. This alternate start, while more exposed, allows you to bypass the chimney and traverse over to the rappel anchors at its top. From here, head left up steep, gravelly ledges and rock steps, generally following a cairned trail that zig-zags its way up the right edge of the snow-filled gully, until blocked by steep cliffs protecting the summit 50 feet from the top of the gully. There are several possible variations.

Descending the Class 3 chimney near the summit.

PHOTO BY GINNI GREER

Scramble to your right until you are able to go up toward a small notch just to the right of the summit block. A couple of variations are also possible here, but expect to find lower fifth-class terrain on any of them.

Once at the notch (J8), traverse up and along the southwest side of the summit block on an exposed ledge until forward progress is blocked by a vertical wall beyond a large, sandy platform. At this point, a Class 3 chimney to the left provides access to the summit. Enjoy the views from the surprisingly large, flat summit (if weather permits).

There are rappel bolts on the summit, but this would require a double-rope rappel. Most retrace the ascent route, using the rope to descend short sections if necessary. Be wary of pulling down loose rock while retrieving the rope. Expect to find three rappel stations, the first being just below the notch in the summit ridge, another a little below this pitch, and the third above the wet chimney at the start of climbing.

6. Pigeon Peak

Pigeon Peak.

ROUND-TRIP DISTANCE	9.5 miles backpacking; 4.4 miles scrambling
ROUND-TRIP TIME	8 hours from camp
STARTING ELEVATION	8,077 feet at Needleton; 11,598 feet at campsite
HIGHEST ELEVATION	13,972 feet
ELEVATION GAIN	4,200 feet backpacking; 4,000 feet scrambling
SEASON	June to September; in June you are likely to find snow in the northwest basin
JURISDICTION	San Juan National Forest, Columbine Ranger District, Weminuche Wilderness
MAPS	Storm King Peak 7.5 minute; Snowdon Peak 7.5 minute

OVERVIEW: A long backpack followed by easy on-and-off trail hiking and a steep scramble to the summit.

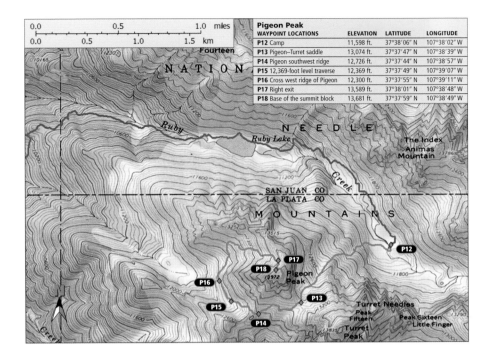

Pigeon Peak				
WAYPOINT LOCATIONS		ELEVATION	LATITUDE	LONGITUDE
P12 Camp		11,598 ft.	37°38′06″ N	107°38′02″ W
P13 Pigeon–Turret saddle		13,074 ft.	37°37′47″ N	107°38′39″ W
P14 Pigeon southwest ridge		12,726 ft.	37°37′44″ N	107°38′57″ W
P15 12,369-foot level traverse		12,369 ft.	37°37′49″ N	107°39′07″ W
P16 Cross west ridge of Pigeon		12,300 ft.	37°37′55″ N	107°39′11″ W
P17 Right exit		13,589 ft.	37°38′01″ N	107°38′48″ W
P18 Base of the summit block		13,681 ft.	37°37′59″ N	107°38′49″ W

GETTING THERE: Take the narrow-gauge railway from Durango or Silverton to Needleton.

COMMENT: Pigeon Peak is one of the most prominent mountains in the Needles area. It can be seen as the train proceeds along the Animas River from Durango.

The route described here climbs from a camp at the head of the Ruby Creek drainage under the east face and around to the northwest face to gain the summit.

On my first foray onto this peak, the final ledges were covered by up to 6 inches of hail (deposited the previous afternoon). This made the ledges quite precarious. New snow in September would also increase the difficulty.

Watch out for the marmots. On one occasion we returned to camp just in time to see three very large critters dragging my backpack out from under the vestibule of the tent.

APPROACH: [See map on page 49.] From Needleton, cross the Animas River via the conveniently located footbridge and hike north along the sometimes hard-to-follow trail on the east bank of the river. This trail

Approaching the second saddle at waypoint P14.

passes several private cabins before entering a series of grassy meadows. At P1, there is a large tree across the trail with its center section cut out. Here the Noname Trail diverges from the Ruby Creek Trail. Just beyond the log, head first northeast then southeast in a small meadow before entering the trees at P2. This is the start of the Ruby Creek Trail, and it may be marked by small branches on the ground forming an arrow. From here, the trail is cairned.

Follow the trail as it heads first southeast then starts a long, rising, northeast traverse at P3. The trail crosses a small ridge before turning east into a small drainage. The trail crosses this drainage at P4 and climbs steeply on poor footing generally northeast to the nose of another small ridge. The trail crosses this ridge and then drops down to a 6-foot down-climb (P5). It is very easy to miss this when descending the trail. If you miss this step on the way back, you can wander endlessly on cairned trails that go nowhere that you want to be.

From the step at P5, the trail contours around to a small saddle on the ridge (P6). The trail divides here, with the right fork heading south over the saddle. Don't take this. (It may be closed with branches. This is the old

Ascend the shallow basin northwest of the summit.

trail, which peters out quite quickly.) Take the left fork that traverses generally east to waypoint P7, where our trail is joined by a lower trail. On your return, remember to take the upper trail at P7. The trail heads generally east now through more open woodland, reaching a clearing at P8. There is a confusing mess of trails in this area, so just traverse across this boulder field as best you can to the point at the eastern edge of the boulders where you can regain the trail at P9. Try to stay on the trail as it heads east along the south side of Ruby Creek before crossing the creek at P10, just below the outlet of the small lake to the east of Ruby Lake.

From here, the trail follows the northern edge of Ruby Lake and continues eastward for a short distance before climbing steeply north to waypoint P11. The trail continues to climb steeply as it heads southeast through high willows, eventually skirting the northeast edge of the large meadow that is your camping destination. A good camp can be found near P12, close to the southeast end of the meadow.

Be assured that this is the nastiest backpack you will encounter in this guidebook.

The Class 3 slot angling up and right provides access through the initial difficulties of the summit block.

ROUTE DESCRIPTION: From camp (P12), climb west, then southwest, using the steep, cairned trail that starts below the cliff band, reaching the Pigeon-Turret saddle at 13,074 feet (P13).

Head west on a descending traverse to a small saddle on Pigeon's southwest ridge (P14), sometimes finding a faint trail that may help.

From here, descend on a trail that hugs the right side of the basin northwest into the scenic basin west of Pigeon Peak.

When you reach the 12,369-foot level (P15), contour north until you have rounded the west ridge of Pigeon and can see into the shallow basin northwest of the summit block (P16).

Do an ascending traverse on faint trails north-northeast into the basin on grassy slopes while avoiding the slabs, then cut back to the east on one

On the ramp after exiting the Class 3 slot.

of the many social trails, aiming for a point below the north cliffs guarding the summit. This will bring you into the upper part of a loose, gravelly gully that you climb until you are able to exit to the right at about 13,600 feet (P17). Scramble up to the base of the summit block (P18).

The summit block provides fun Class 3 or Class 4 scrambling on ledge systems. There are several possible routes. The photo on page 62 shows a Class 3 slot we followed until we were able to exit left onto a ramp, marked by cairns.

Several cairned routes lead to the summit, so if you want to use the same route for the descent, take note of which line you used.

To descend, reverse the route, possibly detouring at the Pigeon-Turret saddle to bag Turret Peak on the way back. The route is straightforward.

Middle Cimarron

The Middle Fork of the Cimarron River.

The Middle Fork of the Cimarron provides easy access to the Big Blue Wilderness, one of the most scenic areas in the state. Surrounded by spectacular peaks, the terrain is quite open and rolling. The peaks are dotted around the generally rolling terrain. From the pass between Heisshorn and El Punto, the hiker is rewarded with spectacular views of Uncompahgre Peak, Wetterhorn Peak, Coxcomb and many others.

History

Dwight Lavender and Forrest Greenfield made first ascents of El Punto and Heisshorn during the 1929 Colorado Mountain Club outing to the Lake City area, both in one day. The summit ridge on El Punto caught their attention, as did the ridge on Heisshorn, which they found to be quite challenging. Lavender wrote about Heisshorn, "As a difficult climb, Heisshorn remains in our memories of this outing second only to Coxcomb."

Lavender and Greenfield would also have had the first ascent of Coxcomb on the same outing, but they were stopped by the notch in the summit ridge. Note, however, that they were able to ascend and descend the challenging Class 4 chimney that provides access to the summit ridge. Two days after this attempt, Henry Buchtel and a party of seven climbed the peak equipped with "rope, hammer, and metal spikes." (Information provided by *Trail and Timberline*, Number 132, October 1929.)

The volcanic origins of this area can be clearly seen in this photo of Precipice Mountain.

THE ROCK

This part of the San Juans is characterized by volcanic rock. The tuff, deposited as ash, creates the striking colors and loose, crumbly rock of the area.

7. Coxcomb

Clouds stream off the summit of Coxcomb Peak.

ROUND-TRIP DISTANCE	8 miles backpacking; 4.2 miles climbing
ROUND-TRIP TIME	6 to 7 hours from camp (C1)
STARTING ELEVATION	10,049 feet at the trailhead; 11,458 feet at camp (C1)
HIGHEST ELEVATION	13,656 feet
ELEVATION GAIN	1,500 feet backpacking; 2,600 feet climbing
SEASON	July to October
JURISDICTION	Uncompahgre National Forest, Ouray Ranger District, Big Blue Wilderness
MAPS	Wetterhorn Peak 7.5 minute; Courthouse Mountain 7.5 minute

OVERVIEW: A short backpack, a moderate trail approach to scrambling, and two difficult Class 4 sections. Rappel a mid-Class 5 notch that must be climbed on the way back.

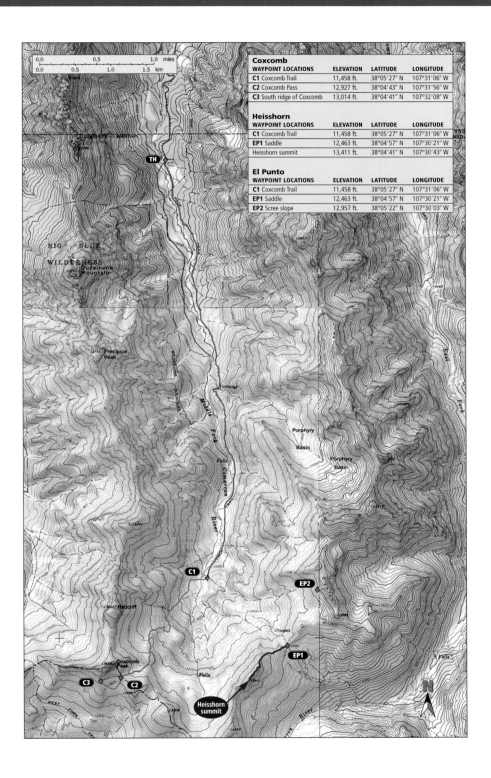

| **Coxcomb** | | | |
WAYPOINT LOCATIONS	ELEVATION	LATITUDE	LONGITUDE
C1 Coxcomb Trail	11,458 ft.	38°05′27″ N	107°31′06″ W
C2 Coxcomb Pass	12,927 ft.	38°04′43″ N	107°31′56″ W
C3 South ridge of Coxcomb	13,014 ft.	38°04′41″ N	107°32′08″ W

| **Heisshorn** | | | |
WAYPOINT LOCATIONS	ELEVATION	LATITUDE	LONGITUDE
C1 Coxcomb Trail	11,458 ft.	38°05′27″ N	107°31′06″ W
EP1 Saddle	12,463 ft.	38°04′57″ N	107°30′21″ W
Heisshorn summit	13,411 ft.	38°04′41″ N	107°30′43″ W

| **El Punto** | | | |
WAYPOINT LOCATIONS	ELEVATION	LATITUDE	LONGITUDE
C1 Coxcomb Trail	11,458 ft.	38°05′27″ N	107°31′06″ W
EP1 Saddle	12,463 ft.	38°04′57″ N	107°30′21″ W
EP2 Scree slope	12,957 ft.	38°05′22″ N	107°30′03″ W

Approximate route of the trail to Coxcomb Pass is shown in red.

GETTING THERE: From U.S. 50, turn south 18.5 miles west of Sapinero, 2.5 miles east of Cimarron on the road to Silver Jack Reservoir (Big Cimarron Road). The sign says 21 miles to the reservoir. Continue past the reservoir and 0.7 mile past the Jackson Ranger Station to a junction where the East Fork Road takes off on the left. Stay on the main road toward Owl Creek Pass. The road crosses the river on a single-lane bridge, and the Middle Fork Road turns left immediately after the bridge. Follow the reasonable Middle Fork Road south. Stay to the left at a junction after 1.8 miles. (The right fork would take you across the river and not to the trailhead.) The road ends at the trailhead after 4.7 miles.

It is also possible to approach the Middle Fork of the Cimarron by going over Owl Creek Pass from U.S. 550. This road takes off from U.S. 550 north of Ridgway and reaches the Middle Fork turnoff in 21.5 miles.

COMMENT: One of the most famous non-Fourteeners in the San Juans, this peak is generally considered to be one of the most difficult of the Bicentennials to climb by its easiest route.

Coxcomb is prominent on the skyline driving south on U.S. 550; it is one of the most spectacular ridgelines in the state.

The peak is normally approached via the West Fork of the Cimarron River. This involves driving as far as possible up the West Fork Road

Looking over to Coxcomb's south ridge; aim for the grassy slopes just below the rock band.

(sometimes to be stopped by a stream crossing), then hiking on the West Fork Trail over the pass to the north of Coxcomb, dropping down to about 12,200 feet before starting to climb a southwest-facing gully.

The route described here offers an alternate approach that combines well with climbs of Heisshorn and El Punto. It also offers a much more pristine environment. It joins the normal route high on Coxcomb's south flank.

APPROACH: From the Middle Fork Trailhead (TH), follow the good trail for 4.0 miles to its junction with the Coxcomb Trail (C1). There are good camping spots around here.

ROUTE DESCRIPTION: From the junction of the Middle Fork Trail and the Coxcomb Trail, take the Coxcomb Trail to Coxcomb Pass (C2) on the southeast shoulder of Coxcomb. This trail is not always easy to follow across the meadow but can be seen as it starts to ascend grassy slopes above the meadow.

At the pass, the trail descends via switchbacks into the large and scenic Wetterhorn Basin. Depending on how you feel about traversing talus slopes, either contour directly across to Coxcomb's south ridge or drop down about 200 feet on the trail and cross to the south ridge on grassy slopes.

On reaching the south ridge, you will find a grassy bench above the first

Descending the south ridge below the alcove used to climb the summit block.

rock band. You can either take this or aim for the slightly lower level. Either way, go left around the corner (C3) on faint climbers' trails, and ascend directly on solid rock and talus to the base of the summit block. An obvious alcove is the target.

Climbing the short step into the alcove.   PHOTO BY GINNI GREER

Climb into the alcove via a short, Class 4 step and scramble up to the base of the upper chimney.

Depending on conditions, this chimney can be climbed with crampons, rock shoes, or just with boots. It holds ice well into July, and when Charlie Winger and I first climbed it in the late 1980s, it was full of ice. Since we didn't have crampons, we climbed something further to the left. I don't, however, recommend this, since it was Class 5 and extremely loose.

In good conditions, this chimney is hard Class 4.

Climbing the upper chimney to the summit ridge.

PHOTO BY GINNI GREER

When icy or wet, it quickly becomes more serious and is usually roped.

Once you are at the top of the chimney, scramble up on a climbers' trail to the top of the ridge and head along the quite narrow ridge toward the summit. A notch in the ridge will quickly stop you. Rappel this 20-foot notch and leave the rope in place for the return trip (set it up as a top-rope with locking carabiners).

Climb up the far side of the notch (Class 4), and it is a short walk to the summit.

Reverse the route to descend, top-roping the notch (mid-Class 5), and head back to the top of the chimney.

In July 2004, there were two large rappel anchors. The anchor directly at the head of the chimney allows you to rappel on a 50-meter rope, but the potential exists for stuck ropes and rockfall when pulling the rope. An anchor to the right (as you descend) appears to be a cleaner rappel, but you may need a longer rope, so be careful. If you have two ropes with you, this is definitely a better rappel.

Preparing to rappel the notch in the summit ridge.

8. "Heisshorn"—Unnamed 13,411

Approaching the Heisshorn-El Punto saddle. Heisshorn is to the right, with Wetterhorn behind.

ROUND-TRIP DISTANCE	8 miles backpacking; 3.4 miles scrambling
ROUND-TRIP TIME	3 hours from camp (C1)
STARTING ELEVATION	10,049 feet at the trailhead; 11,458 feet at camp (C1)
HIGHEST ELEVATION	13,411 feet
ELEVATION GAIN	1,500 feet backpacking; 1,900 feet climbing
SEASON	July to October
JURISDICTION	Uncompahgre National Forest, Ouray Ranger District, Big Blue Wilderness
MAPS	Wetterhorn Peak 7.5 minute; Courthouse Mountain 7.5 minute

OVERVIEW: A short backpack into the Middle Fork Basin; moderate trail hike to a pass with a steep, difficult scramble on extremely loose rock.

SEE MAP PAGE 67

GETTING THERE: From U.S. 50, turn south 18.5 miles west of Sapinero, 2.5 miles east of Cimarron on the road to Silver Jack Reservoir (Big Cimarron Road). The sign says 21 miles to the reservoir. Continue past the reservoir and 0.7 mile past the Jackson Ranger Station to a junction where the East Fork Road takes off on the left. Stay on the main road toward Owl Creek Pass. The road crosses the river on a single-lane bridge, and the Middle Fork Road turns left immediately after the bridge. Follow the reasonable Middle Fork Road south. Stay to the left at a junction after 1.8 miles. (The right fork would take you across the river and not to the trailhead.) The road ends at the trailhead after 4.7 miles.

It is also possible to approach the Middle Fork of the Cimarron by going over Owl Creek Pass from U.S. 550. This road takes off from U.S. 550 north of Ridgway and reaches the Middle Fork turnoff in 21.5 miles.

APPROACH: From the Middle Fork Trailhead (TH), follow the good trail for 4.0 miles to its junction with the Coxcomb Trail (C1). There are good camping spots around here.

Starting up the ridge.

ROUTE DESCRIPTION:
From the junction with the Coxcomb Trail (C1), hike for 1.2 miles on a good trail to the saddle between Heisshorn and El Punto (EP1).

Gary climbing the slabs below the summit.

As the trail becomes fainter in the meadows below the pass, follow wooden posts to arrive at the saddle. The views into the East Fork Valley are spectacular, with excellent views of Uncompahgre, Wetterhorn, and Matterhorn peaks.

At the saddle, turn right and hike on grassy slopes to the base of the ridge proper. As you engage the ridge, stay on the crest as much as possible. The lichen-covered rock is extremely slippery when wet.

The ridge is quite narrow in spots as you approach the final summit block. At one point you will follow a faint trail that takes you to the left side of the ridge before heading back to the crest on talus. This section is quite loose, especially after heavy rainfall. The summit block has a short, slabby section before becoming extremely unstable for the rest of the ascent. Test each handhold and foothold in this section.

To descend, reverse the route.

Carefully descending loose blocks on the ridge.

9. "El Punto"—Unnamed 13,280

El Punto seen from Heisshorn.

ROUND-TRIP DISTANCE	8 miles backpacking; 4 miles climbing
ROUND-TRIP TIME	5 hours from camp (C1)
STARTING ELEVATION	10,049 feet at the trailhead; 11,458 feet at camp (C1)
HIGHEST ELEVATION	13,280 feet
ELEVATION GAIN	1,500 feet backpacking; 1,800 feet climbing
SEASON	July to October
JURISDICTION	Uncompahgre National Forest, Ouray Ranger District, Big Blue Wilderness
MAPS	Wetterhorn Peak 7.5 minute; Courthouse Mountain 7.5 minute

OVERVIEW: A short backpack into the upper Middle Fork Basin, a trail hike to a pass. A scramble on talus and scree to the summit block, with a short, steep climb on loose rock to a tiny summit. Some will prefer to use a rope for the final section.

SEE MAP PAGE 67

GETTING THERE: From U.S. 50, turn south 18.5 miles west of Sapinero, 2.5 miles east of Cimarron on the road to Silver Jack Reservoir (Big Cimarron Road). The sign says 21 miles to the reservoir. Continue past the reservoir and 0.7 mile past the Jackson Ranger Station to a junction where the East Fork Road takes off on the left. Stay on the main road toward Owl Creek Pass. The road crosses the river on a single-lane bridge, and the Middle Fork Road turns left immediately after the bridge. Follow the reasonable Middle Fork Road south. Stay to the left at a junction after 1.8 miles. (The right fork would take you across the river and not to the trailhead.) The road ends at the trailhead after 4.7 miles.

It is also possible to approach the Middle Fork of the Cimarron by going over Owl Creek Pass from U.S. 550. This road takes off from U.S. 550 north of Ridgway and reaches the Middle Fork turnoff in 21.5 miles.

Climb the scree and talus slope at left in this photo, aiming for the obvious gully that goes up to the left shoulder of the peak.

Scrambling up the gully to reach the left shoulder.

COMMENT: This peak has been described as "a smaller version of Lizard Head Peak." Certainly, the summit block has the same aiguille-like appearance and is similarly composed of fractured volcanic rock. The climbing, however, is only Class 3. A rope is good to have though, because of the loose rock, although it may be a challenge to find a placement that is any good.

The exposed summit is often climbed by belaying one person at a time over to the true summit.

Climbing the summit block.   PHOTO BY GINNI GREER

Belaying the summit, one at a time.   PHOTO BY GINNI GREER

APPROACH: From the Middle Fork Trailhead (TH), follow the good trail for 4.0 miles to its junction with the Coxcomb Trail (C1). There are good camping spots around here.

ROUTE DESCRIPTION: From the junction with the Coxcomb Trail (C1), hike for 1.2 miles on a good trail to the saddle between Heisshorn and El Punto (EP1). From the saddle, turn north and follow the ridge until it provides access to the grassy slopes below the peak. Aim for the central scree and talus slope (EP2), and head for a shoulder on the left side of the summit block.

Once you are on the shoulder, it is a short, Class 3 scramble up the summit block, followed by an intimidating 20-foot traverse to the actual summit. The best way to climb to the true summit is to traverse on a ledge, just on the right side of the ridge. The ridge crest is extremely loose.

Downclimb or rappel off the summit block (good rappel anchors are not plentiful) and return to camp.

Ouray-Silverton Area

Looking back down the valley from Ice Lake.

There's enough good climbing in this area to keep us going for a long time. Think of this as a sampler. The scrambles described here are all accessed from U.S. 550. Four-wheel-drive roads are plentiful in this area, largely due to the heavy mining activity that has occurred here.

History

The earliest climb of any of the routes in this guide probably occurred in this area. In *Trail and Timberline* (Number 157, November 1931), Dwight Lavender used a little detective work to conclude that the first ascent route of Mount Sneffels, in September 1874, by Rhoda, Wilson, Endlich, and Ford, was in fact the southwest ridge route described in this guide. Since then, this route has become much less popular than the Lavender Col route used here for descent.

Ice Lake Basin was "attacked" by the Colorado Mountain Club during its 1932 outing, with no less than six first ascents claimed by Dwight Lavender in his trip report (*Trail and Timberline*, Number 168, October 1932). While it appears that at least two of the peaks had been climbed previously (Vermillion Peak in 1874 and Golden Horn in July 1932 by a group of students from Michigan School of Mines), it is likely that first ascents of several peaks were achieved, including Pilot Knob and U.S. Grant. According to William H. Bueler's *Roof of the Rockies*, Engineer Mountain was first climbed in 1873 by H. G. Prout.

Ice Lake Basin is definitely one of my favorite places in the entire state. I have spent quite a bit of time here, either on day climbs from the car or preferably having camped for a few days. Fantastic slopes of red, gold, and purple cascade down from the peaks on three sides, a sign of the unstable, crumbling rock characteristic of the area. Camping by Ice Lake allows several peaks to be climbed in relatively short days, allowing time in the afternoons to relax and soak up the wilderness.

Colorful scree on the peaks ringing Ice Lake Basin.

THE ROCK

The volcanic origins of much of the San Juans are nowhere as obvious and spectacular as they are in this area. The tuff creates a colorful, unstable landscape.

10. U.S. Grant

U.S. Grant, seen from the summit of Pilot Knob.

ROUND-TRIP DISTANCE	3.4 miles from Ice Lake; 8.8 miles from Ice Lake Trailhead
ROUND-TRIP TIME	3 hours from Ice Lake; 6 hours from Ice Lake Trailhead
STARTING ELEVATION	9,827 feet at trailhead; 12,265 feet at camp
HIGHEST ELEVATION	13,767 feet
ELEVATION GAIN	1,500 feet from Ice Lake; 4,000 feet from trailhead
SEASON	June through September
JURISDICTION	San Juan National Forest, Columbine Ranger District
MAP	Ophir 7.5 minute

OVERVIEW: An enjoyable climb characterized by one short, difficult section close to the summit that may require use of a rope.

GETTING THERE: Two miles northwest of Silverton on U.S. 550, take the South Mineral Creek Road (County Road 7) for 4.5 miles to a parking area directly across the road from the South Mineral Campground (TH).

COMMENT: This peak has a reputation as one of the most difficult of the top 200 peaks in Colorado. In fact, most of the climb is very straight-forward, with a short, difficult section near the summit that may require a rope. The climb is very doable from a camp at Ice Lake. The first time I climbed this peak was when Charlie Winger completed the Bicentennials. We waited to open the champagne until we had descended this tricky step.

APPROACH: From the west end of the parking area, take the excellent Ice Lake Trail for 3.5 miles and 2,500 feet of elevation gain to Ice Lake, passing Lower Ice Lake at 2.3 miles. Immediately after passing the lower lake, the trail heads through a scenic rock band guarding the upper basin, revealing a spectacular view.

U.S. Grant from above Ice Lake. Note the trail in the foreground. The saddle between U.S. Grant and Peak V4 is just out of sight at left side of photo.

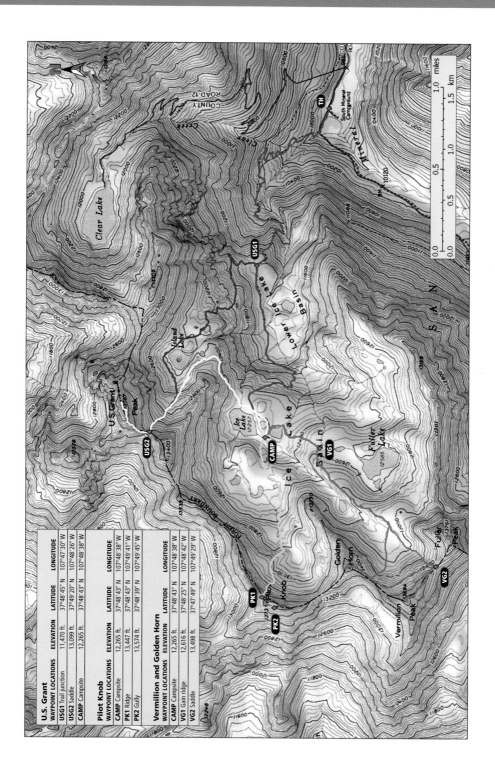

U.S. Grant

WAYPOINT LOCATIONS	ELEVATION	LATITUDE	LONGITUDE
USG1 Trail junction	11,470 ft.	37°48'45" N	107°47'30" W
USG2 Saddle	13,099 ft.	37°49'20" N	107°48'26" W
CAMP Campsite	12,265 ft.	37°48'43" N	107°48'38" W

Pilot Knob

WAYPOINT LOCATIONS	ELEVATION	LATITUDE	LONGITUDE
CAMP Campsite	12,265 ft.	37°48'43" N	107°48'38" W
PK1 Ridge	13,447 ft.	37°48'43" N	107°49'41" W
PK2 Gully	13,574 ft.	37°48'39" N	107°49'45" W

Vermillion and Golden Horn

WAYPOINT LOCATIONS	ELEVATION	LATITUDE	LONGITUDE
CAMP Campsite	12,265 ft.	37°48'43" N	107°48'38" W
VG1 Gain ridge	12,616 ft.	37°48'25" N	107°48'42" W
VG2 Saddle	13,498 ft.	37°47'49" N	107°49'29" W

View of the ridge from the saddle between U.S. Grant and Peak V4.

If you are doing this climb as a day hike from the car, you can use a more direct approach to Island Lake. Initially the same as for Ice Lake, after hiking 1.9 miles from the trailhead, look for a faint trail taking off to your right (USG1). This point is just before you reach Lower Ice Lake and is right after the trail flattens out as it leaves the river canyon. Look for a cairn to mark this point.

The trail rapidly improves and switchbacks up the hill before reaching Island Lake in 1.1 miles. From here, join the route coming over from Ice Lake.

ROUTE DESCRIPTION: From a camp by Ice Lake, pick up a faint trail that contours at the 12,400-foot level to the northeast, around the southeast ridge of Peak 13,520 (unofficially named V4). Follow the trail as it swings to the northwest and bypasses the unique and aptly named Island Lake. It is a straightforward scramble on faint trails, grass, and scree to the saddle (USG2) between U.S. Grant and V4. From the saddle, head north (right) up the ridge on a gravelly trail through the talus.

The trail weaves between some minor gendarmes until it crosses a narrow ridge to a tiny saddle directly below the summit block.

Across the saddle is a 10-foot step. This area is definitely exposed, but the left of the two cracks provides reasonable footholds and handholds, and after two or three moves there is an intermediate ledge. Many parties use a rope here.

A narrow ledge system leads to the right for perhaps 100 feet until a lower-angled gully provides access to the summit area and a short walk brings you to the summit.

Climber at the crux step on the 1st ascent.
CMC ARCHIVES

Downclimbing the final gully with a loose belay.

11. Pilot Knob

Pilot Knob, seen from Golden Horn.

ROUND-TRIP DISTANCE	2.8 miles round trip from Ice Lake; 9.8 miles from Ice Lake Trailhead
ROUND-TRIP TIME	4 to 5 hours from Ice Lake; 8 to 9 hours from Ice Lake Trailhead
STARTING ELEVATION	9,827 feet at trailhead; 12,265 feet at camp
HIGHEST ELEVATION	13,738 feet
ELEVATION GAIN	1,480 feet from Ice Lake; 3,900 feet from Ice Lake Trailhead
SEASON	June through September
JURISDICTION	San Juan National Forest, Columbine Ranger District
MAP	Ophir 7.5 minute

OVERVIEW: A short, stiff climb on generally loose scree, finishing with exposed scrambling on better rock.

SEE MAP PAGE 83

GETTING THERE: Two miles northwest of Silverton on U.S. 550, take the South Mineral Creek Road (County Road 7) for 4.5 miles to a parking area directly across the road from the South Mineral Campground (TH).

COMMENT: Pilot Knob has a reputation as one of the more difficult climbs in the Bicentennials. Perhaps the route has become easier as more parties have climbed it, but I would suggest that the route described here is quite reasonable.

APPROACH: From the west end of the parking area, take the excellent Ice Lake Trail for 3.5 miles and 2,500 feet of elevation gain to Ice Lake, passing Lower Ice Lake at 2.3 miles. Immediately after passing the lower lake, the trail heads through a scenic rock band guarding the upper basin, revealing a spectacular view.

ROUTE DESCRIPTION: From the south end of Ice Lake (CAMP), head west on a faint trail up a shallow draw toward the impressive basin between Pilot Knob and Golden Horn. Contour on the left side of the basin, then gradually gain elevation, heading for a prominent couloir a short distance to the right of a point below the north end of the summit block. This distinctive couloir is bright red and yellow in color. Exit onto the ridge (PK1), staying generally on the right side of this very loose gully. This will put you about 100 feet from the summit block, looking very impressive from this angle.

The summit block of Pilot Knob, seen from the top of the scree couloir used to gain the ridge.

The first time I was on this peak, I headed up the ridge to the base of the summit block, then started

Class 4 gully giving access to the summit ridge.

traversing across the north face. After some time, it became obvious that this line was too high, especially when I saw a climbers' trail perhaps 30 feet below me. This high traverse was quite difficult and had nothing to recommend it beyond the spectacular, geode-looking horizontal crack that provided occasional handholds.

A much better way to traverse the north face is to take the lower trail, which leaves the northeast ridge at a point where the rock color changes from bright red and yellow to a purplish gray—the color of the summit block. It then crosses below the north face to the northwest ridge, turns south, and runs for 150 yards until you reach a weakness in the summit block (PK2). Scramble approximately 50 feet up this gully until you can escape to the left on a series of ledges. A few cairns mark this line, helpful for finding the descent route.

Once you are on the summit ridge, head north. It is a straightforward scramble to the middle summit, followed by a tricky but short downclimb on the way to the north summit. Some parties belay the downclimb off the middle summit, but in fact, while exposed, there are good handholds and footholds.

Descend by reversing the route.

Looking back along the summit ridge. The downclimb from the middle summit can be seen just to the right of the ridge.

12. Vermillion and Golden Horn

Golden Horn (left) and Vermillion Peak.

ROUND-TRIP DISTANCE	4.6 miles from Ice Lake; 11.6 miles from Ice Lake Trailhead
ROUND-TRIP TIME	5 hours from a camp at Ice Lake; 9 hours from the trailhead
STARTING ELEVATION	9,827 feet at the trailhead; 12,265 feet at camp
HIGHEST ELEVATION	13,894 feet
ELEVATION GAIN	2,000 feet from Ice Lake; 4,500 feet from the trailhead
SEASON	June through September
JURISDICTION	San Juan National Forest, Columbine Ranger District
MAP	Ophir 7.5 minute

OVERVIEW: Moderate scrambles on two peaks with an interesting Class 3 descent.

SEE MAP PAGE 83

GETTING THERE: Two miles northwest of Silverton on U.S. 550, take the South Mineral Creek Road (County Road 7) for 4.5 miles to a parking area directly across the road from the South Mineral Campground (TH).

Bypassing an obstacle on Vermillion's ridge.

COMMENT: These two peaks combine well in a day, whether from the Ice Lake Trailhead or from a camp at Ice Lake. While easier than the other routes described, these could be considered a good warm-up if you are camped in Ice Basin for a few days. They are worth the effort.

APPROACH: From the west end of the parking area, take the excellent Ice Lake Trail for 3.5 miles and 2,500 feet of elevation gain to Ice Lake, passing Lower Ice Lake at 2.3 miles. Immediately after passing the lower lake, the trail heads through a scenic rock band guarding the upper basin, revealing a spectacular view.

ROUTE DESCRIPTION: From your Ice Lake camp, follow the continuation of the Ice Lake Basin Trail as it heads over to Fuller Lake. Before reaching Fuller Lake, at waypoint VG1 head right up grassy slopes to join a ridge leading into the basin between Vermillion and

Heading up the loose gully to Vermillion's summit ridge.

Golden Horn from Vermillion.

Fuller. Pick up a cairned trail on this ridge that takes you all the way up to the Vermillion-Fuller saddle.

Turn right and follow a climbers' trail along Vermillion's southeast ridge, skirting difficulties on the left side.

Shortly after the section shown in the upper photo on page 90, you will encounter a loose gully that provides access to the summit ridge. Scramble up this gully to the ridge. From here, it is a walk to the summit. Enjoy the views. Especially take a look at Golden Horn. The route will mostly follow the ridge.

Return to the Vermillion-Fuller saddle. There is a gully that you can take from just below the summit of Vermillion that cuts off a little distance, but it is very loose and probably not worth it.

Once you are at the saddle, descend slightly before taking a faint trail that heads for a bench at the 13,400-foot level. This will take you over to the Vermillion-Golden Horn saddle.

From the saddle, scramble up the ridge, only leaving it briefly to traverse on a ledge on your right before heading back left and continuing to the summit.

To descend, return to the Vermillion-Golden Horn saddle and descend directly down the scree. Carefully downclimb a short section of rock through a cliff band.

Once you are below the cliff band, head back to rejoin the trail.

Looking up at the tricky downclimb below the Vermillion-Golden Horn saddle.

13. Lookout Peak

Lookout Peak is climbed via the ridge on the lefthand skyline.

ROUND-TRIP DISTANCE	2 miles
ROUND-TRIP TIME	3 hours
STARTING ELEVATION	11,716 feet
HIGHEST ELEVATION	13,661 feet
ELEVATION GAIN	2,000 feet
SEASON	Late June through September
JURISDICTION	San Juan National Forest, Columbine Ranger District
MAP	Ophir 7.5 minute

OVERVIEW: A steep scramble on a loose ridge with some challenging route finding on the summit block.

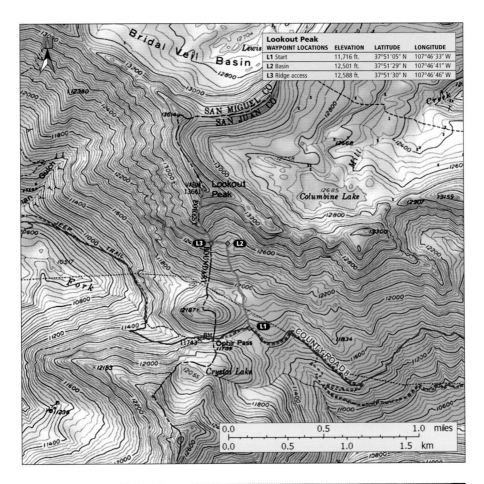

Lookout Peak			
WAYPOINT LOCATIONS	ELEVATION	LATITUDE	LONGITUDE
L1 Start	11,716 ft.	37°51'05" N	107°46'33" W
L2 Basin	12,501 ft.	37°51'29" N	107°46'41" W
L3 Ridge access	12,588 ft.	37°51'30" N	107°46'46" W

GETTING THERE: Drive 5 miles north of Silverton or 17 miles south of Ouray on the Million Dollar Highway, U.S. 550, and turn west on the Ophir Pass Road. The pass can also be reached from the west side, via Ophir, but that road is much rougher.

Follow the Ophir Pass Road for 3.9 miles and

The grassy slopes offer a reasonable way to reach the ridge.

The summit block. The route heads towards the right.

park in a small pull-out on the north side of the road (L1). This parking area is 0.2 mile east of Ophir Pass.

COMMENT: If you have a few spare hours while in the Silverton area, consider this climb. It is a short, fun scramble providing spectacular views from the summit. This peak is in the heart of the San Juans and provides good views of many of the important ranges in this area. It is well named.

APPROACH: The route starts at the car.

ROUTE DESCRIPTION: From the car, follow a faint trail north along the right side of a shallow gully in the general direction of the peak, which is visible the whole way. This gully deposits you in a broad basin immediately to the right (east) of the south ridge of Lookout (L2). From this basin at 12,500 feet, head left toward the south ridge, aiming for a grassy slope that provides reasonable access to the ridge at about 12,600 feet (L3).

Head up the ridge, staying either slightly to the right of the ridge or on the crest of the ridge, where the rock tends to be more solid.

The ridge flattens out just before the summit block. Look for cairns heading to the right for about 50 feet, and follow these as best you can as you ascend a series of gravelly ledges to the summit.

Enjoy the views.

Climbing the ledges of the summit block.

14. The Southwest Ridge of Mount Sneffels

The southwest ridge of Mount Sneffels from the approach to Blue Lakes Pass.

ROUND-TRIP DISTANCE	5.3 miles
ROUND-TRIP TIME	6 hours
STARTING ELEVATION	11,316 feet
HIGHEST ELEVATION	14,150 feet
ELEVATION GAIN	2,700 feet
SEASON	Late June to October
JURISDICTION	Uncompahgre National Forest, Ouray Ranger District
MAP	Telluride 7.5 minute

OVERVIEW: A walk on roads and a trail to Blue Lakes Pass, followed by a Class 3 scramble on progressively better rock to the summit.

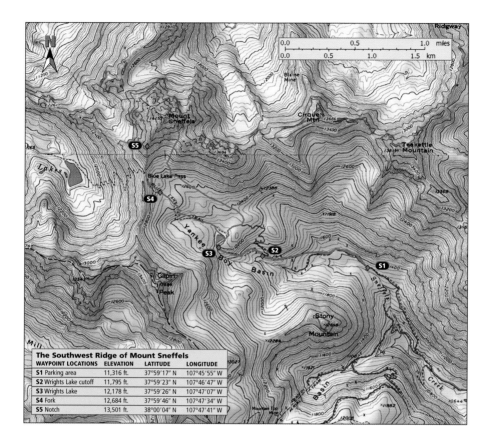

The Southwest Ridge of Mount Sneffels			
WAYPOINT LOCATIONS	ELEVATION	LATITUDE	LONGITUDE
S1 Parking area	11,316 ft.	37°59′17″ N	107°45′55″ W
S2 Wrights Lake cutoff	11,795 ft.	37°59′23″ N	107°46′47″ W
S3 Wrights Lake	12,178 ft.	37°59′26″ N	107°47′07″ W
S4 Fork	12,684 ft.	37°59′46″ N	107°47′34″ W
S5 Notch	13,501 ft.	38°00′04″ N	107°47′41″ W

GETTING THERE: From the town of Ouray, head south on U.S. 550 for 0.3 mile from the south end of Main Street, and turn right onto the Camp Bird Mine Road. Cross the upper bridge over the Box Canyon at 0.4 mile and continue on the dirt road up Canyon Creek to a junction at 4.9 miles (9,620 feet). Take the right fork and head up Sneffels Creek to a parking area at 8.3 miles (S1).

Note that the road becomes progressively rougher as you proceed, and to drive to the parking area mentioned definitely requires a four-wheel-drive vehicle. It is possible to drive considerably further up this road, but are we climbers or four-wheelers? There is an outhouse at the parking area.

COMMENT: Truly a classic, this ridge provides an impressive backdrop to Yankee Boy Basin. The spectacular pinnacles that dominate the lower part of the ridge might scare off the aspiring scrambler, but in fact the only rea-

The ridge, as seen from Blue Lakes Pass.

sonable route bypasses these features quite easily. A climb of any single feature would be an adventure in itself.

The difficulty of this ridge is rated Class 3, but when Ginni and I climbed this route in late July, early monsoon flow and a cold front from the north combined to coat the rock with a layer of verglas (a thin layer of ice). This is a good example of why we take a rope on climbs that might not normally be roped. One crux section felt very much like Class 4 or harder, with boots slipping off small rock features.

ROUTE DESCRIPTION: From the parking area (S1), walk up the road for 0.8 mile to a point where the Wrights Lake Cutoff Trail leaves the road (S2). Take this trail for 0.4 miles to the small lake (S3), where the trail rejoins the road briefly. After perhaps 100 yards, the trail leaves the road and heads around the right side of the lake to Blue Lakes Pass, staying left at the fork (S4). The right fork takes you up the normal ascent route (trail number 204).

At Blue Lakes Pass, take a moment to look at the ridge. You can see that a climbers' trail bypasses the difficulties of the lower ridge on its left (west) side.

Head up the climbers' trail as it hugs the left side of the ridge, climbing on talus. Continue up to the 13,500-foot level (S5), and move right, through a notch. Drop down 20 feet or so and then traverse on ledges into the large, south-facing gully. You can also stay to its left edge, but you will be forced back into the gully eventually (Class 3). Either way, follow the gully to its end before exiting a narrow slot on the right edge. Just follow the climbers' trail in this section.

In the upper notch.

The slot deposits you on the upper ridge. The scrambling from here to the summit is on ledges with very solid rock. Stay either on the ridge or on its right (east) side.

From the summit, pick up the well-used "normal route" trail for the descent. This uses a narrow gully that parallels the east ridge (on its south side) and takes you down to Lavender Col. By the way, Lavender Col provides access to the north face of Sneffels if you're interested in climbing a route there.

From Lavender Col, descend the broad, shallow couloir to the defined trail at its entrance. Follow the trail to the road and head back to the car.

15. Engineer Mountain—Northeast Ridge

Approaching Engineer Mountain.

ROUND-TRIP DISTANCE	6 miles
ROUND-TRIP TIME	4 to 5 hours
STARTING ELEVATION	10,678 feet
HIGHEST ELEVATION	12,968 feet
ELEVATION GAIN	2,300 feet
SEASON	Late June to October
JURISDICTION	San Juan National Forest, Columbine Ranger District
MAP	Engineer Mountain 7.5 minute

OVERVIEW: A short trail approach to a fun ridge scramble. Some Class 3 and maybe a couple of moves of Class 4.

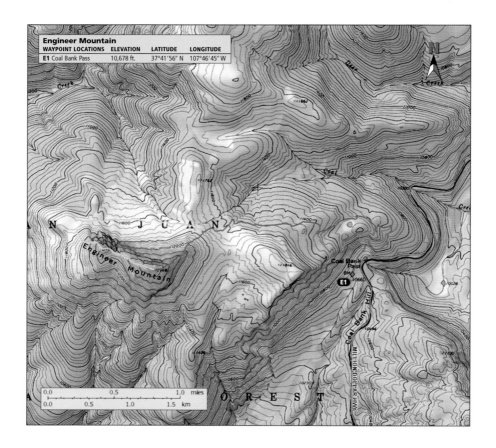

GETTING THERE: Drive to the trailhead at the summit of Coal Bank Pass, 14.3 miles south of Silverton on U.S. 550. The trail leaves from a small parking area on the west side of the highway. The trailhead is just west of Coal Bank Pass and is found via an unmarked dirt road across the highway from the restrooms on the pass.

COMMENT: This is a fun, short scramble on a famous landmark. Driving along U.S. 550 south of Silverton, you have probably seen this peak many times. One of these times you should stop and climb it. It is worth it.

ROUTE DESCRIPTION: From the trailhead at Coal Bank Pass (E1), head up the excellent trail on switchbacks, emerging from the trees at about 11,600 feet into meadows often carpeted with flowers. You will soon reach a trail junction signed for the Engineer Mountain Trail (a different trail). At this junction, take the obvious trail that heads up the northeast ridge, directly in front of you.

Follow the climbers' trail up the ridge—a slippery undertaking. The best trail seems to stay closest to the ridge crest.

The ridge quickly steepens and narrows as you reach a corridor of white rock. Enter the narrow corridor and climb a 10-foot crack system at the end of the corridor, exiting left onto the ridge crest.

The exit cracks may appear difficult, but there are many good handholds and footholds. Some will prefer to rope this short section, especially on the descent.

After regaining the ridge crest, continue up a climbers' trail, mainly on top of the ridge. The views from the top are great—the Grenadiers and Needle Mountains are especially prominent.

Descend by reversing the route. However, if you absolutely must climb the sub-peak (12,613 feet), continue over the sub-peak and descend west along the edge of the rugged and rotten north face, detouring left into a loose, shallow gully when the ridge becomes too steep.

Contour around the north side of the mountain and cross the rock glacier to regain your ascent trail. This alternate descent route is not recommended, since you will have to negotiate large, unstable blocks with significant sliding potential.

The optional descent route is shown in yellow on the map.

Approaching the crux.

San Miguel Range

The northeast ridge of Lone Cone.

The prominent shape of Lone Cone dominates the skyline south of Norwood. Marking the western edge of the San Miguel Range and west of the Wilson Group of Fourteeners, Lone Cone is well named, presenting a solitary, symmetric profile.

Fractured and loose at the start, the rock improves near the top of the ridge of Lone Cone. This photo shows the author high on the route.

PHOTO BY CHARLIE WINGER

THE ROCK

Lone Cone is reported to be an extinct volcano and is largely composed of fractured rock, although in some areas, such as the northeast ridge, there are sections of relatively solid slabs that provide great scrambling.

16. Lone Cone—Northeast Ridge

Approaching Lone Cone's northeast ridge.

ROUND-TRIP DISTANCE	4 miles
ROUND-TRIP TIME	4–5 hours
STARTING ELEVATION	10,681 feet
HIGHEST ELEVATION	12,613 feet
TOTAL ELEVATION GAIN	2,000 feet
SEASON	When the roads are passable, usually sometime in June until snow falls in October
JURISDICTION	Uncompahgre National Forest, Norwood Ranger District
MAPS	Beaver Park 7.5 minute; Lone Cone 7.5 minute

OVERVIEW: A serious ridge scramble with one short section of very loose, fractured rock followed by an incredible ridge with plenty of exposure (Class 4) on solid slabs. A four-wheel-drive vehicle is recommended for the often muddy and sometimes steep, rocky approach roads.

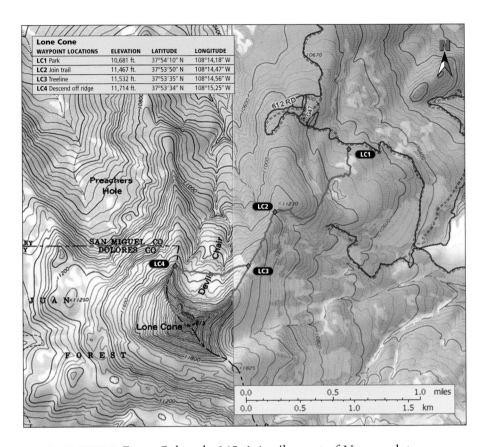

Lone Cone WAYPOINT LOCATIONS	ELEVATION	LATITUDE	LONGITUDE
LC1 Park	10,681 ft.	37°54'10" N	108°14,18" W
LC2 Join trail	11,467 ft.	37°53'50" N	108°14,47" W
LC3 Treeline	11,532 ft.	37°53'35" N	108°14,56" W
LC4 Descend off ridge	11,714 ft.	37°53'34" N	108°15,25" W

GETTING THERE: From Colorado 145, 1.4 miles east of Norwood, turn south on County Road 44Z S (signed as Lone Cone Road). Measuring from this junction, drive south on County Road 44Z S, reaching the U.S. Forest Service boundary at mile 10.3. The road becomes dirt at this point and is designated as Forest Service Road 610. Continue south until you reach Beef Trail Road (County Road M44) at mile 11.6. Turn left (east) on Beef Trail Road. At mile 14, turn right on Forest Service Road 611 (not well signed). At mile 18.9, stay straight at the junction with Beaver Park Road. At mile 20.5, turn right on Forest Service Road 612 and follow this progressively rougher road to the parking spot at mile 24.3, where an old logging road (closed by a downed tree) takes off to the left (LC1). Note that 1.2 miles before the parking area you will pass another road on your left, closed by U.S. Forest Service signs. While this road can also be used to access Lone Cone's northeast ridge, the route finding is more complex and is not recommended.

Negotiating the loose rock of the cockscomb ridge.

COMMENT: Historically the "standard route" was from the northwest, but due to access problems, this side is now difficult to reach. The moderate north ridge is the most reasonable route and is probably the most popular way to climb this peak. As such, it makes a good descent route. The best scrambling route ascends the northeast ridge and is a serious undertaking, sometimes turning back experienced scramblers.

Surrounded by aspen forest, the peak is especially worth a visit during autumn, when it sits on a sea of gold. Once the rough approach roads are snow-covered, they become impassable, so don't wait too long for this one.

APPROACH: From the parking area (LC1), walk generally south then southwest along an old logging road (closed to vehicles) and reach a small pond in 0.3 mile. From the lake, climb steeply to the southwest up forested slopes, following cow trails. Aim for a saddle on the peak's northeast ridge, labeled on the map as 11,230. Another old logging road, not shown on the map, may help you reach this saddle.

Once you are on the ridge, join a faint trail (LC2) and walk southwest up the ridge crest to tree line at 11,532 feet, 1.1 miles from your vehicle (LC3). From this point, you have a good view of the route.

ROUTE DESCRIPTION: From treeline at 11,532 feet, aim for the cockscomb where the ridge narrows dramatically. This section, though short, is quite challenging due to the extremely loose nature of the rock. Test every handhold and foothold, as even large blocks may surprise you.

When you're past this section, the ridge broadens for awhile and becomes mellow; don't be fooled. The upper part of the ridge is superb scrambling on generally sound but steep slabs. Staying on the ridge proper definitely puts you on Class 4 terrain, although some difficulties can be bypassed to the left. Some parties might prefer to use a rope for short sections. Shortly after reaching the prominent point seen in the cover photo, the terrain again moderates. An easy scramble on talus takes you to the summit.

Descend via the north ridge to tree line, at an elevation of 11,714 feet. Use a climbers' trail to descend off the ridge and onto the rock glacier (LC4). Contour across the rock glacier, which forms the seat of the feature known as the Devil's Chair, aiming for tree line on the northeast ridge where you will rejoin your ascent route. Reverse the balance of your ascent route back to your vehicle.

Excellent scrambling on the upper slabs.

Sangre de Cristo Range

Sunrise in winter on the Crestones.

The Sangre de Cristo Range is long, narrow, and steep. Some of the most challenging scrambles in the state can be found here. The relatively solid rock makes this area a favorite of scramblers. Expect plenty of exposure on some of these routes.

Sandwiched between the San Luis Valley on the west and the Wet Valley to the east, the climbs have reasonable access, although driving up the four-wheel-drive roads on either side of the range will test driver and vehicle.

For climbs accessed from the east, the small town of Westcliffe provides amenities.

From the San Luis Valley, a good place to fuel the body for the long backpack in can be found at the Great Sand Dunes Oasis Restaurant, located just outside Great Sand Dunes National Park.

If you have time, practice your telemark turns on the sand dunes.

Conglomerate rock.

PHOTO BY CHARLIE WINGER

THE ROCK

The Crestones are famous for their conglomerate rock, yielding quite solid rock with lots of features. The Precambrian rock of the Blanca Massif also provides good scrambling. Glaciation has sculpted this range into the form seen today.

17. Milwaukee to Pico Asilado

Pico Asilado from Milwaukee Pass.

ROUND-TRIP DISTANCE	7.4 miles from Upper Sand Creek Lake; 7.2 miles backpacking to Upper Sand Creek Lake
ROUND-TRIP TIME	11 hours from Upper Sand Creek Lake
STARTING ELEVATION	11,722 feet from Upper Sand Creek Lake; 10,636 feet from trailhead
HIGHEST ELEVATION	13,611 feet
ELEVATION GAIN	4,700 feet from Upper Sand Creek Lake; 2,230 feet backpacking to Upper Lake, of which 570 feet is climbed on the way out
SEASON	June to October (determined by road opening)
JURISDICTION	Pike and San Isabel National Forest, San Carlos Ranger District; and Great Sand Dunes National Monument and Preserve (National Park Service)
MAPS	Crestone Peak 7.5 minute; Beck Mountain 7.5 minute

OVERVIEW: A difficult scramble and a long day.

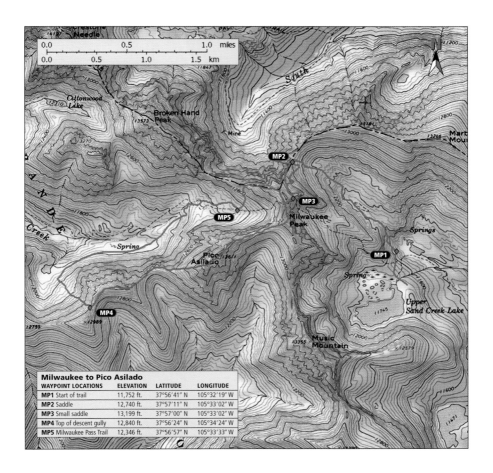

Milwaukee to Pico Asilado			
WAYPOINT LOCATIONS	ELEVATION	LATITUDE	LONGITUDE
MP1 Start of trail	11,752 ft.	37°56′41″ N	105°32′19″ W
MP2 Saddle	12,740 ft.	37°57′11″ N	105°33′02″ W
MP3 Small saddle	13,199 ft.	37°57′00″ N	105°33′02″ W
MP4 Top of descent gully	12,840 ft.	37°56′24″ N	105°34′24″ W
MP5 Milwaukee Pass Trail	12,346 ft.	37°56′57″ N	105°33′33″ W

GETTING THERE: From the town of Westcliffe, head south on Colorado 69 for 4.5 miles. Turn right onto Colfax Lane and head south for 5.5 miles to a T-junction. Make a left turn and follow the road for 5.25 miles to the Rainbow Trailhead. There is a large parking area here where passenger cars should be left. Four-wheel-drive vehicles can continue up the rough road for a further 2.6 miles to another large parking area. As you enter the parking area, you will see a sign for the Music Pass Trail, pointing to the right.

COMMENT: If you have the time, it is worth attempting to combine climbs of Tijeras and Pico Asilado in one trip. In this case, it makes sense to establish a camp at Upper Sand Creek Lake to shorten the climb of Pico Asilado. This adds less than a mile to the relatively short climb of Tijeras. The following description assumes a base camp at Upper Sand Creek Lake.

The ledge on Milwaukee Peak, seen from the notch.

APPROACH: Head up the trail to Music Pass, crossing several berms in the first hundred yards. Reach the pass in 1.25 miles and enjoy the spectacular view of Tijeras, and other peaks. Continue over the pass on the excellent trail to Upper Sand Creek Lake, a total backpacking distance of 3.6 miles one way. Elevation gain to the lake from the parking area is 1,660 feet, with a loss of almost 600 feet as you descend from Music Pass. Remember that you will have to regain this altitude on your way out! See map on page 117.

ROUTE DESCRIPTION: The first thing to remember for this scramble is not to believe the trail locations shown on the USGS map.

From the camping area at the east end of Upper Sand Creek Lake, head north to gain access to the large basin northeast of Milwaukee Peak. There is a trail (not shown on the map) that provides access into this basin. Pick up this trail (MP1) by heading north for approximately a quarter of a mile and descending 200 feet. A faint trail with occasional cairns may help you find this point.

From here, the trail heads generally northwest, staying just to the right of a cliff band along a ramp. Initially easy to follow, the trail becomes

Approaching the face of Pico Asilado—the route starts in the grassy area left of the snow patch.

spotty through the willows but eventually brings you to more open terrain. Head for the obvious saddle (MP2) between Point 13,661 (west of Marble Mountain) and Milwaukee.

From this saddle, the views into the South Colony Lakes drainage and surrounding peaks are amazing.

Head generally west up the ridge until you catch a trail, faint at first but improving rapidly, which takes you to the left just below the ridge crest to a small saddle (MP3). From here, it is a very short walk to Milwaukee Pass.

Leave the trail at the pass and head south toward Milwaukee Peak, dropping immediately into a notch. Climb out of the notch (difficult move) and onto an exposed ledge. Traverse along this ledge around the corner into a gully that provides access to the summit.

From the top of Milwaukee, you can study the next part of the route, over to Pico Asilado.

Head west toward Pico Asilado, staying generally on or to the left side of the ridge. As you approach Pico Asilado, drop off the ridge on its left side, aiming for a grassy area on the lower part of the face.

Scramble up the face, choosing the line of least resistance. I found a reasonable route that traversed generally to the right, hitting the summit ridge a few feet to the right of the summit. Easier lines may exist to the left of the summit. Expect grassy ledges and rock steps, none higher than 6 to 8 feet but occasionally strenuous and slightly technical. Some people may elect to use a rope here.

The views from the top of Pico Asilado are well worth the climb. The view of the Crestones is truly stunning.

You have two choices for the return trip: reverse your route, or continue along the ridge until it is possible to descend into the Cottonwood Creek drainage and head back over Milwaukee Pass.

The former option is certainly shorter and more aesthetic, although the

View from Pico Asilado to Milwaukee showing the Milwaukee Pass Trail in red.

descent of Pico Asilado requires tricky downclimbing or a rappel.

The second option uses the "normal" route for Pico Asilado. This is the route described here.

Take a minute to pick out the trail that descends from Milwaukee Pass into the Cottonwood Creek drainage. You will need to connect with this trail on your way back to the pass. The trail can be seen on the photo, highlighted in red.

From the summit of Pico Asilado, head west down the ridge until you reach 13,500 feet, at which point you have a choice: Drop into a gully that parallels the ridge on its left side, or try the sporting route over a small pinnacle to stay on the ridge proper (hard Class 4). These two routes rejoin each other soon enough.

Continue west along the ridge (it seems endless) over a small summit (13,020 feet) and down to the saddle at 12,840 feet (MP4). This is the head of the loose, ugly descent gully that takes you down toward a lake at 11,820 feet.

Just before you reach the lake, turn toward the east and contour on talus below rock bands and above the trees to rejoin the trail at or before way-

Descent gully. The lake at 11,820 feet can be seen in upper right corner of photo.

point MP5. The photo below shows the route looking back toward the 11,820-foot lake from a point on the trail heading back up toward Milwaukee Pass.

It is essential that you hook up with the trail to go over the pass. The trail climbs steeply to the north a short distance below the head of the valley and switchbacks up to a spectacular traverse that deposits you at the pass.

When I did this route, I was racing an afternoon thunderstorm moving in from the Crestones, attempting to get back over the pass before the weather hit. It made for a bit of excitement and made the already strenuous climb back up to the pass even more so.

From the pass, retrace your steps back to camp. If you are packing out on the same day, you will be one tired hiker by the time you get back to your car.

Looking back at the route. The 11,820 foot lake is nestled in the basin just above treeline.

18. Tijeras Peak

Tijeras Peak.

ROUND-TRIP DISTANCE	5 miles from Upper Sand Creek Lake; 2.7 miles from Lower Sand Creek Lake; 7.2 miles backpacking to Upper Lake; 6.2 miles backpacking to Lower Lake
ROUND-TRIP TIME	5 hours from Upper Sand Creek Lake
STARTING ELEVATION	11,722 feet from Upper Sand Creek Lake; 10,636 feet from trailhead
HIGHEST ELEVATION	13,604 feet
ELEVATION GAIN	2,800 feet from Upper Sand Creek Lake; 2,100 feet from Lower Sand Creek Lake; 2,230 feet backpacking to Upper Lake, of which 570 feet are climbed on the way out; 1,990 feet backpacking to Lower Lake, of which 570 feet are climbed on the way out
SEASON	June to October (determined by road opening)
JURISDICTION	Pike and San Isabel National Forest, San Carlos Ranger District; and Great Sand Dunes National Monument and Preserve (National Park Service)
MAPS	Crestone Peak 7.5 minute; Beck Mountain 7.5 minute

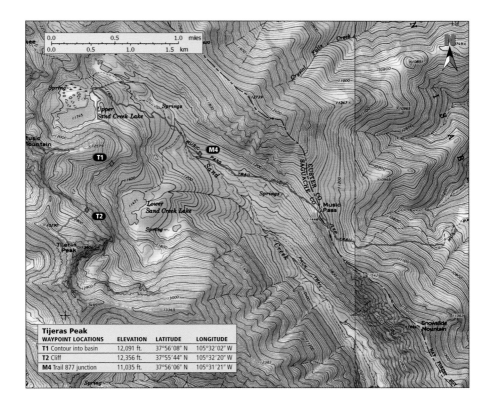

Tijeras Peak			
WAYPOINT LOCATIONS	**ELEVATION**	**LATITUDE**	**LONGITUDE**
T1 Contour into basin	12,091 ft.	37°56'08" N	105°32'02" W
T2 Cliff	12,356 ft.	37°55'44" N	105°32'20" W
M4 Trail 877 junction	11,035 ft.	37°56'06" N	105°31'21" W

OVERVIEW: A moderate scramble with one short, steep section that can hold snow well into July.

GETTING THERE: From the town of Westcliffe, head south on Colorado 69 for 4.5 miles. Turn right onto Colfax Lane and head south for 5.5 miles to a T-junction. Make a left turn and follow the road for 5.25 miles to the Rainbow Trail Trailhead. There is a large parking area here where passenger cars should be left. Four-wheel-drive vehicles can continue up the rough road for a further 2.6 miles to another large parking area. As you enter the parking area, you will see a sign for the Music Pass Trail, pointing to the right.

COMMENT: This climb is accessed via the Music Pass Road. While the area does not see as much climbing traffic as the nearby South Colony Lakes area, the spectacular scenery and excellent fishing do attract quite a number of non-climbers.

The lefthand ramp, providing access through the cliffband.

For a climb of Tijeras Peak alone, you have a couple of options. The climb could be accomplished in a long day from the parking area below Music Pass or by establishing a camp at the east end of Lower Sand Creek Lake.

If you have the time, you may want to combine climbs of Tijeras and Pico Asilado in one trip. In this case, it makes sense to establish a camp at Upper Sand Creek Lake to shorten the climb of Pico Asilado. This adds less than a mile to the relatively short climb of Tijeras. Another combination that works well is Tijeras with Music Mountain (see Scramble 19).

APPROACH: Head up the trail to Music Pass, crossing several berms in the first

Tijeras' summit ridge.

hundred yards. Reach the pass in 1.25 miles and enjoy the spectacular view of Tijeras, and other peaks. Continue over the pass on the excellent trail to Upper Sand Creek Lake, a total backpacking distance of 3.6 miles one way.

ROUTE DESCRIPTION: From the camping area at the east end of Upper Sand Creek Lake, head southeast to a gentle ramp that will take you to the 12,000-foot level on the east ridge of Music Mountain. From here, contour to the southwest, picking your way across talus slopes and through patches of willows. As you cross the ridge and contour into the basin (T1), you will have a clear view of the ramp (T2) that allows access through the rock band (see photo on page 118). Note: An alternate ramp further to the right is described in Scramble 19.

Third-class scrambling brings you to the top of this inset ramp, although with snow on the ramp, conditions may be either easier or more difficult. Note the location of the ramp to allow you to find it again on the descent (several cairns mark this point).

Scramble southwest on grass and talus to a saddle between Tijeras and Point 13,290. From here, follow the ridge southeast to the summit. Stay as close to the ridge crest as possible. Most of the scrambling is Class 3, with one Class 4 move near the top (see photo at right).

On the descent, reverse the route. Or, for a little variation, head down to Lower Sand Creek Lake following a small drainage to the north side of the lake (you may find trails in this section). From the east end of the lake, follow the excellent trail (Number 877) to the junction with the Music Pass Trail (M4). Turn left and follow the trail back to your camp.

Ginni on Tijeras' summit ridge.

19. Music Mountain—South Ridge

Approaching the south ridge of Music Mountain.

ROUND-TRIP DISTANCE	9.5 miles round trip
ROUND-TRIP TIME	10 hours
STARTING ELEVATION	10,705 feet
HIGHEST ELEVATION	13,355 feet
ELEVATION GAIN	3,760 feet
SEASON	June to October (determined by road opening)
JURISDICTION	Pike and San Isabel National Forest, San Carlos Ranger District; and Great Sand Dunes National Monument and Preserve (National Park Service)
MAPS	Crestone Peak 7.5 minute; Beck Mountain 7.5 minute

OVERVIEW: A superb airy scramble on solid rock. Sustained Class 4 or lower-Class 5 scrambling that may require a rope for short sections.

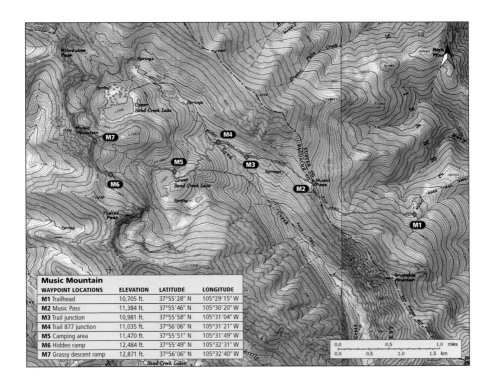

Music Mountain			
WAYPOINT LOCATIONS	**ELEVATION**	**LATITUDE**	**LONGITUDE**
M1 Trailhead	10,705 ft.	37°55'28" N	105°29'15" W
M2 Music Pass	11,384 ft.	37°55'46" N	105°30'20" W
M3 Trail junction	10,981 ft.	37°55'58" N	105°31'04" W
M4 Trail 877 junction	11,035 ft.	37°56'06" N	105°31'21" W
M5 Camping area	11,470 ft.	37°55'51" N	105°31'49" W
M6 Hidden ramp	12,484 ft.	37°55'49" N	105°32'31" W
M7 Grassy descent ramp	12,871 ft.	37°56'06" N	105°32'40" W

GETTING THERE: From the town of Westcliffe, head south on Colorado 69 for 4.5 miles. Turn right onto Colfax Lane and head south for 5.5 miles to a T-junction. Make a left turn and follow the road for 5.25 miles to the Rainbow Trail and Grape Creek trailheads. There is a large parking area here where passenger cars should be left. Four-wheel-drive vehicles can continue up the rough road for 2.6 miles to another large parking area. As you enter the parking area, you will see a sign for the Music Pass Trail, pointing to the right.

COMMENT: The south ridge of Music Mountain calls loudly when viewed from neighboring Tijeras Peak. Unable to find any information on the viability of this route, friends and I explored the ridge during the summer of 2007 and found not only evidence of prior passage but also some outstanding scrambling on amazing rock. With the exception of one short detour, we were able to stay on the ridge proper the whole way on this exposed Class 3 and 4 route. A few bouldery moves are also mixed in to spice things up, so you may want to bring a rope for those sections,

A view of the two gullies leading through the cliff band. The left ramp (more difficult) is described in Scramble 18.

although with dry rock offering great friction, we were comfortable leaving the rope in the pack.

If weather permits, this climb can be combined with Tijeras Peak to create a great loop, although you'll probably want to camp at Lower Sand Creek Lake if you hope to combine them in one day.

APPROACH: From the upper parking area, a good trail climbs 1.2 miles to the top of Music Pass (11,400 feet). Take a break here and enjoy the views of Tijeras Peak, Music Mountain, and Milwaukee Peak. The trail descends more than 400 feet into the Sand Creek drainage, reaching a trail junction at mile 2 (M3). Stay right and continue northwest to a second trail junction at 2.3 miles (M4). For Lower Sand Creek Lake, turn left and almost immediately cross Sand Creek before starting up the gentle switchbacks, reaching Lower Sand Creek Lake at 3.3 miles.

ROUTE DESCRIPTION: To continue on to Music Mountain, skirt around the north side of the lower lake and look for a faint climbers' trail that takes you to tree line in the basin between Music and Tijeras. The cliff band that guards access to the Tijeras-Music ridge can be inspected from here. Either head for the weakness in the cliffs described in Scramble 18 or aim for a second ramp 300 yards to the right (northwest) of the first. This second ramp, hidden from view as you approach it, is quite a bit easier than its neighbor to the southeast

Scrambling on solid rock.

A few sections of the ridge may deserve a rope.

and is more in line with the route up to the south ridge on Music. Take this hidden ramp (M6), which cuts to the left through the cliff band after a short scramble up a scree slope. From the top of the ramp, aim northwest and work your way to the low point of the Tijeras-Music ridge, at the base of Music Mountain's south ridge (12,700 feet).

Start up just to the right of the ridge on grassy ledges and short rock steps until you are forced to the crest of the ridge. Scramble steeply up on wonderful, solid rock until reaching the prominent notch in the ridge just before the south summit. Climbing directly out of the notch requires mid-fifth-class moves, but the difficulties can be skirted on the left side of the ridge. Scramble back up to the ridge and continue to the south summit. Upon reaching the south summit, you'll realize that it's not over yet. The traverse to the north summit, the high point of the peak, requires more scrambling. If you stay close to the ridgeline, the climbing is Class 4, but by dropping a little distance to the southwest of the ridge, it is possible to keep the difficulties to no more than Class 3.

To descend, return to the south summit and head down the steep east ridge on grassy ledges and short rock steps. As the ridge steepens, you will be forced to move to your left (north) to stay on the ridge proper to avoid being cliffed-out.

At an elevation of 12,870 feet, as the ridge starts to flatten out, a grassy ledge allows you to exit the ridge onto the face (M7). Descend talus and grassy slopes back to Lower Sand Creek Lake and rejoin the trail.

Approaching the notch in the south ridge.

20. The Crestone Traverse

The Crestone traverse, seen from Pico Asilado.

ROUND-TRIP DISTANCE	8.6 miles from trailhead (CT2)
ROUND-TRIP TIME	9 to 10 hours
STARTING ELEVATION	11,129 feet
HIGHEST ELEVATION	14,298 feet
ELEVATION GAIN	4,900 feet
SEASON	Late June to October
JURISDICTION	Pike and San Isabel National Forest, San Carlos Ranger District
MAPS	Crestone Peak 7.5 minute, Beck Mountain 7.5 minute

OVERVIEW: A four-wheel-drive road approach; trail hiking to a long, committing Class 3 and 4 scramble above 14,000 feet.

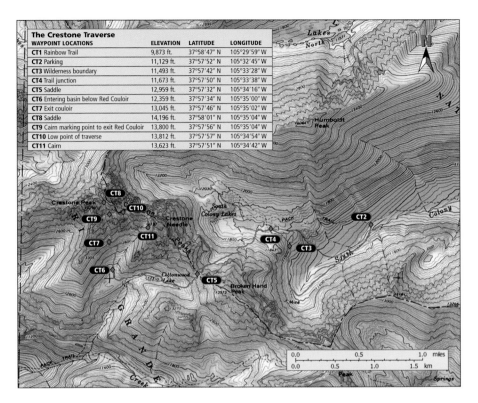

The Crestone Traverse			
WAYPOINT LOCATIONS	**ELEVATION**	**LATITUDE**	**LONGITUDE**
CT1 Rainbow Trail	9,873 ft.	37°58'47" N	105°29'59" W
CT2 Parking	11,129 ft.	37°57'52" N	105°32'45" W
CT3 Wilderness boundary	11,493 ft.	37°57'42" N	105°33'28" W
CT4 Trail junction	11,673 ft.	37°57'50" N	105°33'38" W
CT5 Saddle	12,959 ft.	37°57'32" N	105°34'16" W
CT6 Entering basin below Red Couloir	12,359 ft.	37°57'34" N	105°35'00" W
CT7 Exit couloir	13,045 ft.	37°57'46" N	105°35'02" W
CT8 Saddle	14,196 ft.	37°58'01" N	105°35'04" W
CT9 Cairn marking point to exit Red Couloir	13,800 ft.	37°57'56" N	105°35'04" W
CT10 Low point of traverse	13,812 ft.	37°57'57" N	105°34'54" W
CT11 Cairn	13,623 ft.	37°57'51" N	105°34'42" W

GETTING THERE: From the town of Westcliffe, head south on Colorado 69 for 4.5 miles. Turn right onto Colfax Lane and head south for 5.5 miles to a T-junction. Turn right and either park after 1.5 miles or continue to the trailhead 6.4 miles beyond the T-junction. A warning—the road beyond the parking area has deteriorated over the years. Every time I drive it, I swear it's the last time. Note: at the time of writing the second edition of this guide, the Forest Service had announced that it plans to implement a new road closure and management plan for South Colony Basin. It appears that the new road closure will be located one half mile west of the Rainbow Trail junction, immediately before the first stream crossing. If implemented, this will add 2.5 miles each way to the approach described here.

Contact the San Carlos Ranger District at (719) 269-8704 for current regulations.

COMMENT: How can a guide to classic scrambles not include this one? Good rock, lots of exposure, and challenging route finding combine to make this truly a classic.

Crestone Needle from Broken Hand Pass. The normal route, used here for the descent, follows the gullies.

Approaching the Red Couloir.

It is also very serious. A number of fatalities have occurred on this route, including those of experienced climbers. Escape is not easy, and getting off-route can lead to an epic. The fun Class 3 and 4 climbing can become a nightmare when the route is covered with ice, hail, or snow. A rope is a must for this route, even if you don't plan to use it.

The traverse is often done from Needle to Peak, with a descent down the Peak's north couloir. Doing this bypasses the best scrambling of the route by rappelling the 100-foot descent off the Needle and ends the day with a dangerous descent of the rotten side of the Peak.

The traverse described here is from Peak to Needle, and it maximizes the best rock scrambling and simplifies and shortens the descent at the end of the day.

Starting the traverse.

ROUTE DESCRIPTION: From the trailhead area a mile from the South Colony Lakes (CT2), pass the locked gate and walk along the old four-wheel-drive road. When the road ends, continue on the excellent trail until the Crestone Needle Trail takes off to the left (west) (CT4), passing the Sangre de Cristo Wilderness boundary sign at CT3. Follow this trail (marked with huge cairns) up to the saddle between Broken Hand Peak and Crestone Needle (CT5). To your right is the normal route up the Needle. This will be your descent route, so take a close look at it.

From the saddle, descend on the recently reconstructed trail down to Cottonwood Lake and continue west around the end of the

Approaching the low point of the traverse.

The approximate route on Crestone Needle is shown in red.

Detail showing the route behind the large flake. A climber (circled) can just be seen beyond the flake.

Needle's southwest ridge on a good trail. From here, you have a good view of the south face of the Peak. Locate the prominent red couloir that goes up to a small saddle between Crestone Peak's two summits.

Follow the climbers' trail as it heads up grassy slopes to the right of the couloir, then cuts back and re-enters the couloir above the lower cliff band. Climb in the couloir on solid Class 3 rock (a delight!), then exit onto the rib on the right side (CT7) and scramble up more excellent conglomerate rock until the sides of the couloir start to steepen.

Heading up a gully to the ridge.

Let the cairns guide you back into the upper couloir, then continue on one of the many climbers' trails to the saddle between the two summits (CT8).

The highest of the two summits is to your left (west)—the right summit's claim to fame is as the high point of Custer County. To climb the main summit, scramble on or slightly left of the ridgeline (Class 3).

Now the fun begins. Return to the 14,196-foot saddle. Descend the red couloir back to 13,800 feet. The traverse starts directly opposite a prominent notch on the west side of the red couloir and is marked by a large cairn. Leave the red couloir (CT9) and head east (left) up a loose gully. Follow occasional cairns on the faint climbers' trail as it winds its way up and down and around difficulties.

The trail eventually turns hard to the left and descends to the low point of the traverse, shown in the photo on page 127 (CT10). Descend from this low point and cross the gully to a cairn on its far (east) side (CT11) at an elevation of 13,623 feet. Carefully follow the cairns and traverse to a point where a large, detached flake can be seen. The route climbs behind this flake, seen in the lower photo on page 128.

Climbing the superb summit pitch on the Needle.   PHOTO BY CHARLIE WINGER

At the point where the route turns left in the photos on page 128, you are directly under the huge southwest ridge of the Needle. The route heads left up to the ridgeline in a narrow gully, as shown in the photo on page 129. Just before reaching the ridge, look for a ramp circling around the right side of the next obstacle. Take this and continue to climb up to the base of the final summit tower of the Needle on an expanse of conglomerate rock.

The climb up to the summit is the highlight of the day: solid Class 4 (or perhaps easy Class 5) scrambling for about 100 feet. This is the pitch that is normally rappelled when reversing this route, but the climbing is wonderful, with significant exposure on amazing rock. What could be a better way to finish the traverse?

Carefully descend the Needle's normal route, following the cairned trail.

21. The Little Bear–Blanca Traverse

Looking at the traverse towards Blanca Peak from high on the northwest face of Little Bear Peak.

ROUND-TRIP DISTANCE	10 miles backpacking; 4.4 miles scrambling
ROUND-TRIP TIME	7 to 8 hours scrambling from camp near Como Lake
STARTING ELEVATION	11,929 feet at camp; 8,150 feet at trailhead
HIGHEST ELEVATION	14,345 feet
ELEVATION GAIN	3,800 feet backpacking; 3,200 feet scrambling
SEASON	June through October
JURISDICTION	Rio Grande National Forest, Divide Ranger District; San Isabel National Forest, San Carlos Ranger District
MAPS	Twin Peaks 7.5 minute; Blanca Peak 7.5 minute

OVERVIEW: Backpack approach, with short but steep Class 3 and 4 scramble to the ridge, followed by exposed Class 3 and 4 scrambling along the ridge on excellent rock. Many parties use a rope for a part of this scramble.

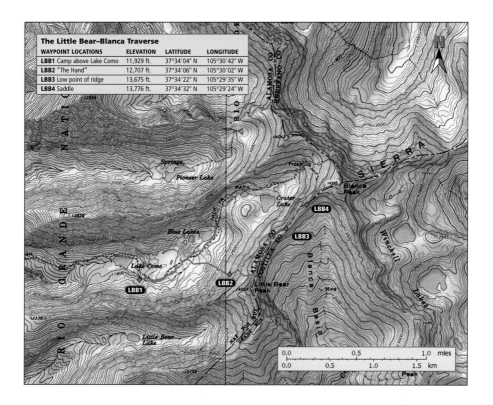

The Little Bear–Blanca Traverse			
WAYPOINT LOCATIONS	ELEVATION	LATITUDE	LONGITUDE
LBB1 Camp above Lake Como	11,929 ft.	37°34'04" N	105°30'42" W
LBB2 "The Hand"	12,707 ft.	37°34'06" N	105°30'02" W
LBB3 Low point of ridge	13,675 ft.	37°34'22" N	105°29'35" W
LBB4 Saddle	13,776 ft.	37°34'32" N	105°29'24" W

GETTING THERE: From the junction of U.S. 160 and Colorado 150 (5.25 miles west of the town of Blanca), drive north on County Road 150 for 3.2 miles to the Lake Como Road. Passenger cars can drive up this road for a little less than 2 miles. There are many parking spots near this point. Four-wheel-drive vehicles may want to drive further up this extremely rough road, but after another mile or two the road becomes the terrain of specialized off-road vehicles (I've seen even these stranded with a bent drive shaft).

COMMENT: What, another Fourteener traverse, you ask? Yes, but what a quality scramble. When combined with the northwest-face approach to Little Bear (which is worth a route in this text by itself), this route has to be one of the best. Long, committing, and challenging, this is a real test piece for scramblers.

APPROACH: From the parking area, hike up the loose road approximately 5 miles to Lake Como. Good campsites can be found a short distance past the lake (LBB1).

ROUTE DESCRIPTION:
From a camp above Lake Como, head up the trail for perhaps 15 minutes, until the northwest face of Little Bear looms over you. Leave the trail on the right and aim for a point (LBB2) to the right of the feature called "the hand," a black stain at the base of the rock face, to the left (north) of the

The northwest face of Little Bear, showing "the hand" (black feature in center of photo). The route starts immediately right of this feature.

summit. There are many possible lines to take, but if you start immediately right of "the hand," you should find a cairned route. Once past "the hand", aim for a low point on the ridge immediately left of Little Bear's summit.

The face is quite committing, and depending on the exact line taken, will expose you to a considerable amount of Class 3 and Class 4 scrambling. If you head further to the right, the difficulty increases dramatically, so stay in the shallow gully that forms the northwest face.

Once you are on the ridge, scramble up a short Class 4 section to the summit of Little Bear.

If the weather looks good, start the long traverse to Blanca Peak. If you don't use a rope, the traverse should take 2 to 3 hours. Using a rope could add several hours to the traverse. Head back down the ridge and have fun. The ridge crest is the place to

On the northwest face of Little Bear.

Climbers on the ridge.

Looking back at "Captain Bivouaco Tower."

PHOTO BY CHARLIE WINGER

be, except for two spots. The first is a small feature called Captain Bivouaco Tower. This is easily passed on either side.

The climbing is exposed and enjoy-able—the rock rea-sonably solid. Very little if any scram-bling harder than Class 4 will be encountered (arguably Class 5.0).

Downclimb a nice knife-edge to the low point on the ridge (LBB3) and approach the crux of the ridge—the tower immediately before LBB4.

Most people bypass this tower by traversing on its right (southeast) side, but the tower can be climbed at lower Class 5.

The author on the catwalk.   PHOTO BY CHARLIE WINGER

LBB4 marks the saddle immediately past this tower. After LBB4, scramble over an exposed catwalk (sometimes called a knife-edge, but it really isn't).

After this catwalk, the difficulties are over. Head to the summit of Blanca and descend on a trail to the Blanca-Ellingwood saddle. The normal route descends from here back to Como Lake.

The Gore Range

Rugged peaks and ridges characterize the Gore Range.

One of the most overlooked ranges in the state—and one providing some of the best scrambling, the Gore Range lies between the northern Park Range and the Ten Mile Range.

Squeezed between Colorado 9 to the east and Interstate 70 to its southwest, this small range has one of the highest concentrations of quality scrambles in Colorado. Since none of the peaks in the Gores is above 13,560 feet (Mount Powell), many peak-baggers have left this area alone.

The peaks are unofficially named, for the most part, after letters of the alphabet, starting with peaks named in 1932 by Carl Erickson and Edmund Cooper, first ascensionists on several major peaks in this area.

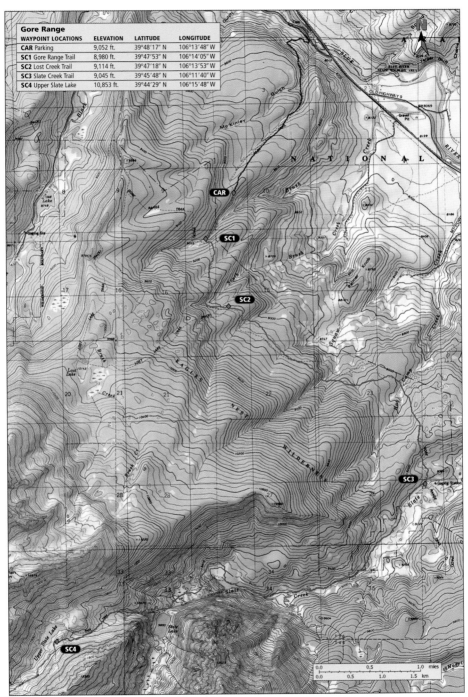

Gore Range			
WAYPOINT LOCATIONS	**ELEVATION**	**LATITUDE**	**LONGITUDE**
CAR Parking	9,052 ft.	39°48'17" N	106°13'48" W
SC1 Gore Range Trail	8,980 ft.	39°47'53" N	106°14'05" W
SC2 Lost Creek Trail	9,114 ft.	39°47'18" N	106°13'53" W
SC3 Slate Creek Trail	9,045 ft.	39°45'48" N	106°11'40" W
SC4 Upper Slate Lake	10,853 ft.	39°44'29" N	106°15'48" W

The backpacking approach for routes 22, 23, and 24.

The first significant climb in the Gore Range was probably that of Mount Powell in 1868 by Ned Farrell and Major John Wesley Powell. This occurred the year before Powell's epic descent of the Colorado River. Much more historical information can be found in William H. Bueler's *Roof of the Rockies*.

Little mining was done in this area, so roads and good trails are few and far between. Expect to do some bushwacking.

Steep and complex, the ridges of the Gore Range offer plenty of scrambling.

THE ROCK

A mixture of metamorphic schist and gneiss along with granite at the southern end of the Gore Range. The range has been heavily glaciated, as evidenced by the cirques and sharp ridges.

22. "Peak Q"—Unnamed 13,230

The moon setting over Peak Q.

ROUND-TRIP DISTANCE	20.4 miles backpacking; 5.2 miles scrambling from camp
ROUND-TRIP TIME	9 hours from Upper Slate Lake camp
STARTING ELEVATION	10,853 feet at Upper Slate Lake; 9,052 feet at Brush Creek Trailhead
HIGHEST ELEVATION	13,230 feet
ELEVATION GAIN	3,900 feet backpacking (1,000 feet of which is gained on the way out); 2,700 feet scrambling from camp
SEASON	Late June to October
JURISDICTION	White River National Forest, Holy Cross and Dillon Ranger Districts, Eagles Nest Wilderness
MAPS	Squaw Creek 7.5 minute; Willow Lakes 7.5 minute; Vail East 7.5 minute

OVERVIEW: A long backpack to a camp near Upper Slate Lake, a bushwhack to "South American Lake," followed by challenging Class 3 and 4 scrambling requiring good route-finding skills.

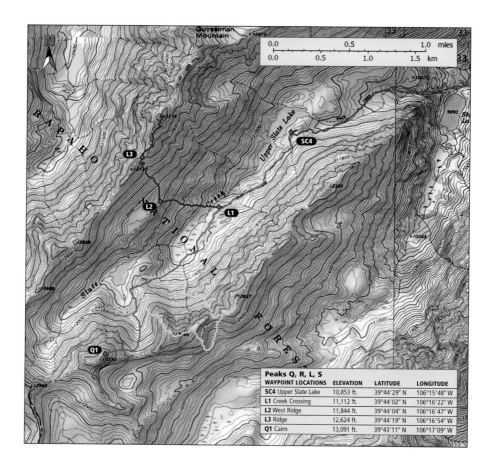

Peaks Q, R, L, S			
WAYPOINT LOCATIONS	**ELEVATION**	**LATITUDE**	**LONGITUDE**
SC4 Upper Slate Lake	10,853 ft.	39°44'29" N	106°15'48" W
L1 Creek Crossing	11,112 ft.	39°44'02" N	106°16'22" W
L2 West Ridge	11,844 ft.	39°44'04" N	106°16'47" W
L3 Ridge	12,624 ft.	39°44'19" N	106°16'54" W
Q1 Cairn	13,091 ft.	39°43'11" N	106°17'09" W

GETTING THERE: Drive north on Colorado 9 from Silverthorne for 16 miles. Turn left on Heeney Road (County Road 30) and drive 0.6 mile to a rough road on the left (opposite Pioneer Cemetery). Cars can be left at the cemetery parking area, or you can drive up this steep, potentially muddy, four-wheel-drive road for 2.4 miles to the Brush Creek Trailhead.

COMMENT: This is one of three climbs in the Slate Creek drainage described in this book. The remoteness of the area means that it really makes sense to combine several climbs in one trip (unless you are a real masochist).

The area is pristine even by Gore Range standards. Over a popular holiday such as the Fourth of July, you may not see any other people in here. Although the backpack into Upper Slate Lake is long and arduous, the scrambling that awaits you is well worth the effort.

View looking up to the saddle between Q and R, with the east ridge of Peak Q at right.

Peak Q dominates the valley. In fact, it stands out from almost anywhere in the Gores. Expect snow on this climb even into July, necessitating the use of crampons (as well as an ice ax) for that alpine start.

CAIRN

The route on Peak Q is shown in red.

APPROACH: See map on page 137. Access to the east side of the Gore Range has become more of a problem over the years, as previously available access points have been closed by property owners. This means that getting to the Slate Creek Trail

Exiting the Class 4 section onto the east ridge of Peak Q.

involves a long approach via the Gore Range Trail either from Brush Creek to the north or Rock Creek to the south. The Brush Creek approach seems to be a little better, since the elevation gained on the way out is less than with the Rock Creek approach (though it is still painful). I will describe the Brush Creek approach.

From the Brush Creek Trailhead, head southwest on a good trail for 0.6 mile to the junction with the Gore Range Trail (SC1). Follow the Gore Range Trail generally south for 4.4 miles to the junction with the Slate Creek Trail (SC3), passing the Lost Creek Trail after 1 mile (SC2). An old cabin is located near the Slate Creek trail junction.

Turn southwest on the Slate Creek Trail and follow it for 5.2 miles to Upper Slate Lake (SC4). Camping spots are few and far between, but try to find one that is off the trail and at least 100 feet from the lake. It is possible to continue on to find more campsites beyond the lake, but bushwhacking with a backpack isn't my idea of a good time.

ROUTE DESCRIPTION: For the climb, head up the valley to the unnamed lake at 11,545 feet (unofficially called South American Lake because of its shape). Slightly before you reach the lake, turn south, heading toward the saddle between Peak Q and Peak R.

Just before reaching the saddle, turn west and scramble up the face, keeping the east ridge on your left. This face holds snow well into July.

Head up until you reach a minor ridge coming off the east ridge. Cross this minor ridge below a cliff and turn left into a narrow couloir that takes you to the east ridge below another cliff band.

Look for a ramp on the right side of this cliff that takes

Approaching the summit block.

you to a point marked by a large cairn, just before crossing the top of the north couloir.

Once you reach the large cairn (Q1), back up about 10 feet and scramble up a short, steep section on the left to reach the ridge again (Class 4). From here, it is a simple scramble up to the base of the summit block, staying to the left side of the ridge.

What appears to be the summit block is now in front of you. Scramble up this block using a steep, narrow gully to gain the ridge top. Descend slightly into a notch and climb steeply upward out of the 10-foot notch to gain the true summit. You may decide to rappel into the notch on the descent.

Reverse the route to descend.

23. "Peak L"—Unnamed 13,213

Peak L.

ROUND-TRIP DISTANCE	20.4 miles backpacking; 4.2 miles scrambling from a camp near Upper Slate Lake
ROUND-TRIP TIME	6 hours from camp
STARTING ELEVATION	10,853 feet at camp; 9,052 feet at Brush Creek Trailhead
HIGHEST ELEVATION	13,213 feet
ELEVATION GAIN	3,900 feet backpacking (1,000 feet of which is gained on the way out); 2,500 feet scrambling from camp
SEASON	Late June to October
JURISDICTION	White River National Forest, Holy Cross and Dillon Ranger Districts, Eagles Nest Wilderness
MAPS	Squaw Creek 7.5 minute; Willow Lakes 7.5 minute; Vail East 7.5 minute

OVERVIEW: A long backpack to a camp near Upper Slate Lake; approach on grassy slopes with a Class 3 traverse along a knife-edge ridge to the summit block and a challenging Class 4 scramble up the face.

SEE MAP PAGE 140

GETTING THERE: Drive north on Colorado 9 from Silverthorne for 16 miles. Turn left on Heeney Road (County Road 30) and drive 0.6 mile to a rough road on the left (opposite Pioneer Cemetery). Cars can be left at the cemetery parking area, or you can drive up this steep, potentially muddy four-wheel-drive road for 2.4 miles to the Brush Creek Trailhead.

COMMENT: Another fine peak in the Slate Creek drainage. This must rate as my favorite peak in the Gore Range. Solid rock and challenging route finding on an impressive-looking peak combine to make this a fine scramble.

APPROACH: For the approach, see the Peak Q approach.

ROUTE DESCRIPTION: From Upper Slate Lake, head west up the drainage on a faint trail (easy to lose in the marshy areas along the lake) until reaching point L1. Cross the creek here and ascend the obvious grassy slope to intersect the shallow gully descending from the west ridge of Peak L at L2. Use this shallow gully to reach the ridge.

Meet the ridge at 12,624 feet (L3) and

Heading up grassy slopes after crossing the creek.

The author on the fine knife edge, on the way to the summit block. PHOTO BY DAN BERECK

cross behind (north side) the first ridge point to a flat area below the horizontal knife-edge that forms the base of the "L". Scramble up to the ridge and traverse across a fun Class 3 knife-edge to the end of this section of ridge.

Study the face before you and notice ramp systems that can provide access to the summit ridge. Downclimb to the base of the summit block and choose a route.

When Dan Bereck and I climbed this peak, we each found different lines. I started on the left side of the summit block and took a right-trending ramp, while Dan dropped down to the right a little way and started in a right-facing dihedral. We both ended up in the same spot: in the dihedral perhaps 40 feet up. At this point, we were forced to make a Class 4 move left out of the dihedral above a large flake. After this, our paths diverged again, with Dan going up a few feet and then traversing to the right into the middle of the face. I moved further left and got into some interesting terrain (read lower Class 5) before again traversing right to rejoin Dan. From this point, some cairns marked a reasonable route to the ridge, generally heading up and right into a shallow, left-facing dihedral. Once you are at the ridge, scramble left along this ridge to the summit.

Be sure to take a rope; it is easy to get into terrain that is difficult to reverse. Old slings bear testament to the fact that on the descent it may be expeditious to rappel one or more sections, although with good route finding it is certainly possible to downclimb the route.

Descend the way you came up.

Downclimbing after the knife edge.

Take a look at the face and choose your route. The right-trending ramp offers one possible line.

Now take a look at these faces—fellow climbers in the Gore Range.

24. "Peak R"— Unnamed 12,995 & "Peak S"—Unnamed 12,857

The north ridge of Peak R. The route starts on the right side of the ridge.

ROUND-TRIP DISTANCE	20.4 miles backpacking; 5.6 miles scrambling from a camp near Upper Slate Lake
ROUND-TRIP TIME	10 hours from camp
STARTING ELEVATION	10,853 feet at camp; 9,052 feet at Brush Creek Trailhead
HIGHEST ELEVATION	12,995 feet
ELEVATION GAIN	3,900 feet backpacking (1,000 feet of which is gained on the way out); 3,100 feet scrambling from camp
SEASON	Late June to October
JURISDICTION	White River National Forest, Holy Cross and Dillon Ranger Districts, Eagles Nest Wilderness
MAPS	Squaw Creek 7.5 minute; Willow Lakes 7.5 minute; Vail East 7.5 minute

OVERVIEW: A long backpack to a camp near Upper Slate Lake. Climb grassy ledges and scramble to the ridge and summit. A tricky downclimb from Peak R to the saddle between R and S followed by a straightforward scramble along the Peak S summit ridge. Descent is via the couloir between R and S.

SEE MAP PAGE 140

Starting up the right side of the north ridge of Peak R.

GETTING THERE: Drive north on Colorado 9 from Silverthorne for 16 miles. Turn left on Heeney Road (County Road 30) and drive 0.6 mile to a rough road on the left (opposite Pioneer Cemetery). Cars can be left at the cemetery parking area, or you can drive up this steep, potentially muddy four-wheel-drive road for 2.4 miles to the Brush Creek Trailhead.

COMMENT: These two peaks are also climbed from the Slate Creek drainage. They are easier than peaks Q and L but still make a good outing, with some challenging route finding.

APPROACH: For the approach, see the Peak Q approach.

ROUTE DESCRIPTION: From Upper Slate Lake, head west up the valley to near "South American Lake." This puts you at the base of the north ridge of

Debby looking at the ledge system leading to a point just below the saddle between Peaks R and S.

Peak R. Head around the right side of the ridge and find grassy slopes and ledges that allow access to a shallow gully that parallels the ridge on its right side.

This grassy gully provides good access to the upper part of the north ridge, traversing around minor ridges before heading up to the ridge crest about 100 feet below the summit. From here, it is a simple scramble up the ridge to the summit.

To climb Peak S from Peak R, start down the easy ridge toward Peak S until a notch makes progress much more difficult. Drop southeast along the edge of the gap to a point at 12,400 feet, where it is possible to down-climb to a ledge system that contours over to a point just below the Peak R–Peak S saddle (shown on the map as a dashed yellow line). When we did this traverse, snow blocked the descent to this ledge, forcing us to descend quite a bit further on steep terrain before being able to cut back to the saddle. Later in the season this shouldn't be a problem.

Head up the slopes to the right of the saddle and gain the ridge. Turn right (east) and scramble over to the summit, staying just left (west) of the ridgeline to avoid some spires.

To descend, head back to the Peak R–Peak S saddle and descend the north couloir. By the way, this couloir is the normal ascent gully if you are climbing Peak S by itself.

Looking back down the summit ridge of Peak S.

The snow couloir at left is the descent gully between Peaks R and S.

25. The Grand Traverse

The Grand Traverse, seen from the east. North Traverse Peak is at left, Grand Traverse Peak to the right.

ROUND-TRIP DISTANCE	11 miles
ROUND-TRIP TIME	10 hours
STARTING ELEVATION	8,622 feet
HIGHEST ELEVATION	13,079 feet
ELEVATION GAIN	5,700 feet
SEASON	June to October
JURISDICTION	White River National Forest, Holy Cross, and Dillon Ranger Districts, Eagles Nest Wilderness
MAPS	Vail East 7.5 minute; Willow Lakes 7.5 minute

OVERVIEW: Good trails in Bighorn Canyon and Deluge Canyon bracket a challenging ridge run requiring good route-finding abilities to keep the difficulty at no more than Class 4.

GETTING THERE: From the East Vail exit from Interstate 70 (exit 180), drive east along the frontage road 2.2 miles to a small parking area (this is the trailhead for the Deluge Lake Trail and the Gore Range Trail). Leave a vehicle

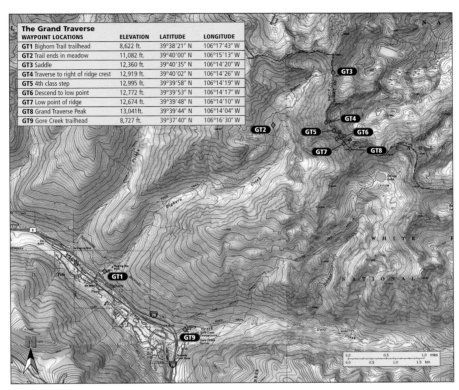

The Grand Traverse			
WAYPOINT LOCATIONS	**ELEVATION**	**LATITUDE**	**LONGITUDE**
GT1 Bighorn Trail trailhead	8,622 ft.	39°38'21" N	106°17'43" W
GT2 Trail ends in meadow	11,082 ft.	39°40'00" N	106°15'13" W
GT3 Saddle	12,360 ft.	39°40'35" N	106°14'20" W
GT4 Traverse to right of ridge crest	12,919 ft.	39°40'02" N	106°14'26" W
GT5 4th class step	12,995 ft.	39°39'58" N	106°14'19" W
GT6 Descend to low point	12,772 ft.	39°39'53" N	106°14'17" W
GT7 Low point of ridge	12,674 ft.	39°39'48" N	106°14'10" W
GT8 Grand Traverse Peak	13,041 ft.	39°39'44" N	106°14'04" W
GT9 Gore Creek trailhead	8,727 ft.	39°37'40" N	106°16'30" W

Leaving North Traverse Peak.

The Class 4 step at waypoint GT5.

The downclimb immediately after waypoint GT5.

here and return 1.6 miles along the frontage road to Columbine Drive. Take this north, under a small underpass to the Bighorn Trail trailhead.

COMMENT: The aptly named "Grand Traverse" crosses the rugged skyline at the head of Bighorn Canyon and is very visible from the town of Vail. The traverse takes in two peaks, unofficially known as "North Traverse Peak" (13,079 feet) and "Grand Traverse Peak" (13,041 feet). This route offers the opportunity to visit two of the most scenic canyons in the Gore Range. In the fall, these canyons can be quite stunning with their aspen-laden hillsides.

APPROACH: This route goes in either direction. Here it is described from north to south. Using two vehicles facilitates the climb, since 1.6 miles separate the two trailheads.

Hike 3.25 miles on the excellent trail up Bighorn Canyon, heading generally northeast. At this point, pass a cabin and continue on a

This tower, reached after negotiating the crux tower at GT5, is best bypassed to the right.

The low point of the traverse (12,674 feet) and next gendarme, bypassed on its right side.

False summit.

trail that stays well above the drainage (on its left side) into the upper basin.

ROUTE DESCRIPTION: Where the trail peters out in a meadow at about 11,100 feet (GT2), contour/climb gradually toward the obvious saddle at the head of the drainage (GT3). A moderate climb on grassy slopes will get you there.

From the saddle, follow the ridge south to the top of "North Traverse Peak," a moderate scramble that is, at most, Class 3.

The summit of "North Traverse Peak" offers great views of the Gore Range, and from here you can contemplate the ridge ahead of you. Allow two to two and a half hours for the ridge-run from "North Traverse Peak" to "Grand Traverse Peak."

The traverse starts out with fun, easy scrambling on solid rock, and route finding is not much of an issue until you reach GT4 after 20 minutes. At this point, it is necessary to drop off the ridge to the right and traverse a few feet below the ridge.

Continue for another 15 minutes to the next difficulty, a tower at GT5 that can be climbed directly (Class 4). An interesting downclimb (see photo on page 154) awaits you on the far side of this spire.

Bypass the next obstacle (see upper photo on page 155) on its right side. An obvious notch on the right side of the ridge looks as if it might afford passage, but it is better to drop another 50 feet to a series of ledges that then allow access back to the ridge. Descend to the 12,674-foot low point (GT7). Drop down to the right until you can cross the gully. From here, traverse past the next gendarme via grassy slopes on its right side (see lower photo on page 155).

The next ridge point looks as if it may be the summit of "Grand Traverse Peak," but, in fact, it is a false summit that again can best be skirted on the grassy slopes to the right.

The final summit block offers a simple scramble. The difficulties are over. Enjoy the view back to the north peak.

Descend the long, somewhat tedious slope southeast to Deluge Lake. Join the excellent trail and descend for 4 miles to the trailhead. Note that the trail has been re-routed from that shown on the topo map quads.

You will briefly join the Gore Creek Trail before reaching the parking area.

Looking back at the traverse.

26. "West Partner Peak"— Unnamed 13,041—South Ridge

The South Ridge of West Partner Peak.

ROUND-TRIP DISTANCE	10 miles
ROUND-TRIP TIME	9 hours
STARTING ELEVATION	8,441 feet
HIGHEST ELEVATION	13,041 feet
ELEVATION GAIN	4,600 feet
SEASON	Late June to October
JURISDICTION	White River National Forest, Holy Cross, and Dillon Ranger Districts, Eagles Nest Wilderness
MAP	Vail East 7.5 minute

OVERVIEW: An easy trail approach with moderate scrambling on solid rock, becoming progressively more interesting as the summit is approached.

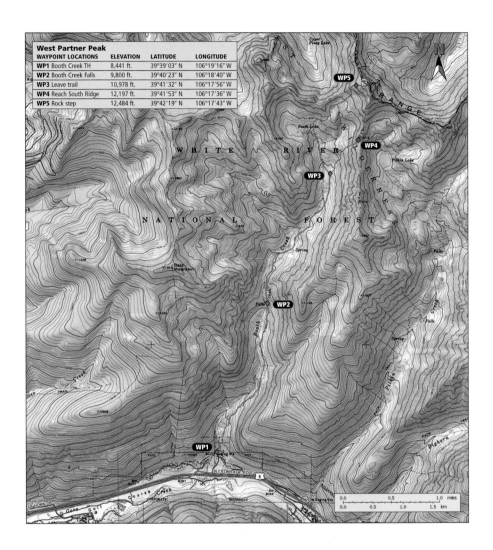

West Partner Peak			
WAYPOINT LOCATIONS	**ELEVATION**	**LATITUDE**	**LONGITUDE**
WP1 Booth Creek TH	8,441 ft.	39°39'03" N	106°19'16" W
WP2 Booth Creek Falls	9,800 ft.	39°40'23" N	106°18'40" W
WP3 Leave trail	10,978 ft.	39°41'32" N	106°17'56" W
WP4 Reach South Ridge	12,197 ft.	39°41'53" N	106°17'36" W
WP5 Rock step	12,484 ft.	39°42'19" N	106°17'43" W

GETTING THERE: From exit 180 on Interstate 70 (East Vail exit), head west on the frontage road for 0.9 mile to Booth Creek Road. Turn right. The Booth Creek Trailhead is 0.2 mile up this road (WP1).

COMMENT: This is another excellent scramble accessed from the East Vail exit, taking you into the heart of the southern Gore Range.

APPROACH: From the trailhead (WP1), follow the Booth Creek Trail for 3.5 miles, passing the popular Booth Creek Falls at 1.8 miles (WP2).

The ascent gully.

ROUTE DESCRIPTION: After 3.5 miles on the trail, leave the trail (WP3) and head northeast towards an obvious gully that provides access to the south ridge.

After reaching the ridge top (WP4), turn north and walk along the easy ridge to the first gendarmes, which can be bypassed on the left side via a good ramp.

Enjoy solid Class 3 scrambling, passing the intersection with the connecting ridge to unofficially named "East Partner Peak." The climbing remains enjoyable right up to the summit.

The west ridge provides a reasonable descent route. Walk down the talus

A view of the ridge from the top of the ascent gully.

to 12,484 feet (WP5), where a step will force you off the ridge proper to grassy slopes on its left side. From the tarn, descend to Booth Lake and rejoin the trail at WP3 for the hike back to the trailhead. By the way, ascending the west ridge directly from its low point is a fine Class 3 or harder scramble if you stay near the ridge crest.

Bypassing some initial gendarmes via a ramp. Pitkin Lake can be seen in the background.

Running the upper ridge.

27. "East Partner Peak"— Unnamed 13,057

An early season approach.

ROUND-TRIP DISTANCE	11 miles
ROUND-TRIP TIME	9 hours
STARTING ELEVATION	8,451 feet
HIGHEST ELEVATION	13,057 feet
ELEVATION GAIN	4,600 feet
SEASON	June to October
JURISDICTION	White River National Forest, Holy Cross, and Dillon Ranger Districts, Eagles Nest Wilderness
MAP	Vail East 7.5 minute

OVERVIEW: A pleasant trail hike to Pitkin Lake followed by a scramble to the ridge. Class 3 climbing on solid rock leads to the summit.

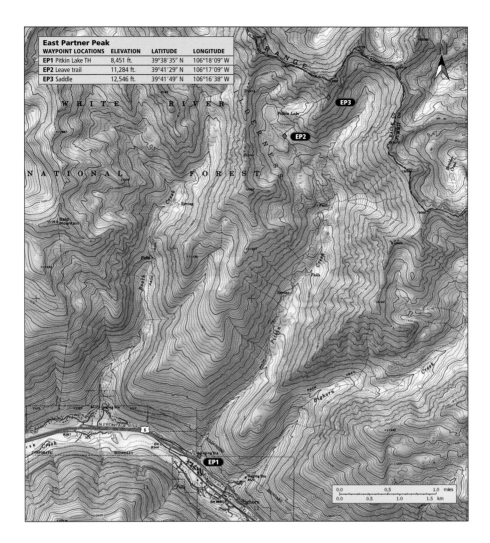

East Partner Peak			
WAYPOINT LOCATIONS	ELEVATION	LATITUDE	LONGITUDE
EP1 Pitkin Lake TH	8,451 ft.	39°38'35" N	106°18'09" W
EP2 Leave trail	11,284 ft.	39°41'29" N	106°17'09" W
EP3 Saddle	12,546 ft.	39°41'49" N	106°16'38" W

GETTING THERE: Take the East Vail exit (exit 180) from Interstate 70. Drive east along the frontage road for a quarter mile to a small trailhead parking area at the Pitkin Lake Trailhead (EP1).

COMMENT: Another enjoyable Gore Range scramble in the heart of the range, with fine views of many other peaks.

APPROACH: From the Pitkin Lake Trail trailhead (EP1), hike 4.4 miles on a good trail until shortly before Pitkin Lake (EP2). Don't leave the trail too soon or you will have to climb up an intervening ridge to reach the basin.

View of the south ridge. The gully providing access to the low point is at the right side of the photo.

Dan on the lower part of the ridge.

ROUTE DESCRIPTION:
Head northeast into the basin below the south ridge. A shallow couloir can be seen that provides access to the low point of the ridge. Head toward this gully, probably on snow in June.

Climb the gully to the ridge on loose talus. From this saddle (EP3), turn left

Traversing from the left side of the final rock rib on a narrow ledge.

and view the ridge. It is a combination of grassy ledges and smooth slabs. Start on a ledge system just to the right of the ridge before working your way back onto the ridge crest.

Just before reaching the summit, several rock ribs must be bypassed on their right side, until the last rock rib is reached. Start up the left edge of this rock rib for 20 feet until a ledge allows passage to the right side of the rib.

From here, it is a straightforward scramble to the summit.

For the descent, reverse the route.

Gerry traversing snow patches below the summit.

28. "Peak C"—Unnamed 13,200

The prominent snow couloir between Peak C and its sub-peak to the right is the normal ascent route. The route described here follows the right-trending finger of snow to the left of the couloir before intersecting the summit snowfield.

ROUND-TRIP DISTANCE	10.3 miles
ROUND-TRIP TIME	11 hours
STARTING ELEVATION	9,360 feet
HIGHEST ELEVATION	13,200 feet
ELEVATION GAIN	4,300 feet
SEASON	June to October
JURISDICTION	White River National Forest, Holy Cross, and Dillon Ranger Districts, Eagles Nest Wilderness
MAPS	Vail East 7.5 minute; Vail West 7.5 minute; Mount Powell 7.5 minute

OVERVIEW: A fine early-season steep snow climb. Later in the season, a good, steep rock scramble.

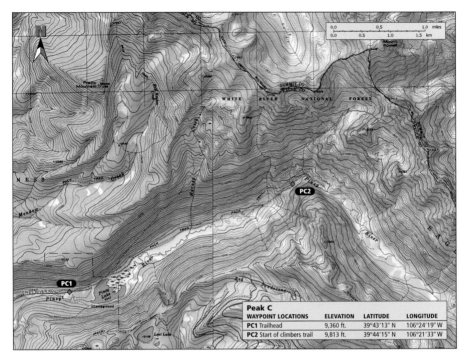

Peak C			
WAYPOINT LOCATIONS	**ELEVATION**	**LATITUDE**	**LONGITUDE**
PC1 Trailhead	9,360 ft.	39°43'13" N	106°24'19" W
PC2 Start of climbers trail	9,813 ft.	39°44'15" N	106°21'33" W

The southwest ridge of Peak C. The snow gully in the center of the photo provides access to this ridge.

GETTING THERE: Take the Main Vail exit (exit 176) off Interstate 70 and drive one mile west along the frontage road to Red Sandstone Road. Turn right (north) and follow the road for 11 miles to a parking area (PC1) immediately before the entrance to the Piney River Ranch.

Starting up the narrow gully on the south face of Peak C. The mixed section can be seen jogging to the right—into the upper part of the gully.

COMMENT: Perhaps the jewel of the Gore Range, Peak C is an imposing mountain as you approach it from Piney Lake. Lower but more rugged than its neighbor, Mount Powell, this peak offers several worthwhile routes. The northwest ridge offers a technical challenge, while the southwest face presents several options for Class 4 scrambling and steep snow climbs.

   The normal route on the southwest face ascends a prominent couloir until it is possible to exit near its end. Almost by accident, Dan Bereck and I found a more direct route up the face that provided excellent, steep snow and mixed climbing, finally taking us on snow directly to the summit. This variation is described here.

APPROACH: From the parking area (PC1), take the trail northeast, avoiding the private land around the lake. After 2.9 miles (PC2), a cairn marks the point where a faint climbers' trail heads north (left). Take this trail, staying on the west side of the stream. The trail is difficult to follow at times as it leads up into the very scenic bowl between Mount Powell and Peak C at 11,200 feet.

ROUTE DESCRIPTION: From this bowl, the route ascends the easternmost gully on the southwest ridge, shown in the photo on page 167. In June, this is moderate snow.

   From the top of this gully, enjoy good views of Kneeknocker Pass, the low point between Peak C and its neighbor to the north, Mount Powell. At 13,580 feet, Mount Powell is the highest point in the Gore Range and makes a good scramble from Kneeknocker Pass along its south ridge.

Also from this point on the southwest ridge, the impressive southwest face of Peak C can be seen clearly. The traditional route follows a descending traverse into the prominent gully hidden from view when looking from the saddle. The more direct, but steeper, route described here is clearly visible in the center of the face.

Topping out onto the summit snowfield. Note the significant cornice.   PHOTO BY DAN BERECK

The gully is steep, and by June the center section may be melted out, providing some good mixed climbing. It is best to be on this early in the morning when you have good cramponing snow. Beware that early in the season the gully is protected by a sizable cornice, which is easily bypassed on the left.

Above the gully, the summit snowfield stretches in front of you. Follow it as it angles left to the summit.

For the descent, retrace your steps. Evaluate snow conditions before descending. A rope may be needed to pass the trickier mixed sections. The normal route provides an alternate descent route.

The upper snowfield leads all the way to the summit.

29. Gore Range Traverse— Eagles Nest to Mount Powell

The long traverse from Eagles Nest to Mount Powell. The east ridge of Eagles Nest is on the right in this photo.

DISTANCE	14.9 miles
TIME	14 hours
STARTING ELEVATION	8,596 feet
HIGHEST ELEVATION	13,560 feet
ELEVATION GAIN	7,100 feet
ELEVATION LOSS	6,320 feet
SEASON	September is probably the best month for this route, when you are likely to have stable weather. Check the weather forecast and wait for a bluebird day.
JURISDICTION	White River National Forest, Holy Cross and Dillon Ranger Districts, Eagles Nest Wilderness
MAPS	Mount Powell 7.5 minute; Vail East 7.5 minute; Vail West 7.5 minute

OVERVIEW: A very long day consisting of many miles of on-trail and off-trail hiking and sustained Class 3 and 4 scrambling for many hours along a high ridge.

GETTING THERE: Surprise Lake Trailhead: From the Silverthorne exit (exit 205) off Interstate 70, drive north on Colorado 9 for 16 miles. Turn left on Heeney Road (County Road 30). Drive 5.6 miles along the west side of Green Mountain Reservoir to the Cataract Creek Road. Turn left and take this graded road for 2.3 miles to the Surprise Lake Trailhead and parking area (on the left). This is a U.S. Fee Area.

   Piney Lake Trailhead: Take the Main Vail exit (exit 176) off I-70 and drive one mile west along the frontage road to the Red Sandstone Road. Turn right (north) and follow the road for 11 miles to a parking area (PC1) immediately before the entrance to the Piney River Ranch.

COMMENT: This may just be the ultimate ridge traverse, long and continuously interesting. With 7,100 feet of elevation gain and many miles of challenging scrambling, the complete traverse may be more than many folks want. For the hardy (or foolhardy), though, the route done in its entirety is extremely satisfying. A rather lengthy car shuttle is required to set this scramble up, unless you can convince friends to help out.

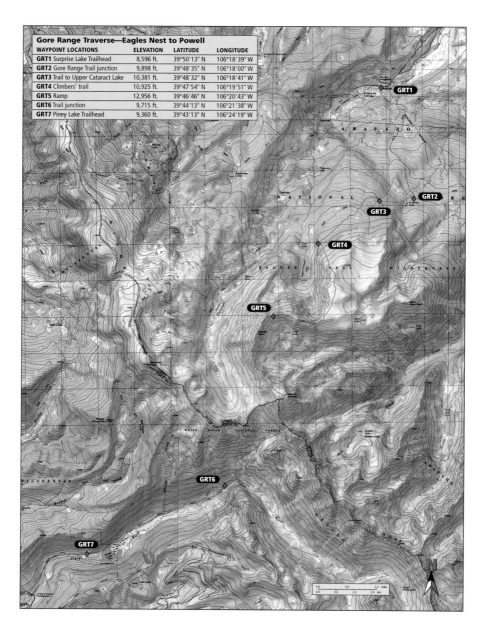

Gore Range Traverse—Eagles Nest to Powell			
WAYPOINT LOCATIONS	**ELEVATION**	**LATITUDE**	**LONGITUDE**
GRT1 Surprise Lake Trailhead	8,596 ft.	39°50′13″ N	106°18′39″ W
GRT2 Gore Range Trail junction	9,898 ft.	39°48′35″ N	106°18′00″ W
GRT3 Trail to Upper Cataract Lake	10,381 ft.	39°48′32″ N	106°18′41″ W
GRT4 Climbers' trail	10,925 ft.	39°47′54″ N	106°19′51″ W
GRT5 Ramp	12,956 ft.	39°46′46″ N	106°20′43″ W
GRT6 Trail junction	9,715 ft.	39°44′13″ N	106°21′38″ W
GRT7 Piney Lake Trailhead	9,360 ft.	39°43′13″ N	106°24′19″ W

For those looking for a slightly shorter day, it is possible to join or leave (depending on the direction you are heading) the Eagles Nest–Powell ridge at its low point, drop into the spectacular basin between Powell and Elliott Ridge, and cut over the saddle southwest of Powell (between Powell and the Cataract Points).

Starting up the east ridge of Eagles Nest.

APPROACH: Take the Surprise Lake Trail from the parking area, crossing a footbridge before climbing steadily as it heads south to the junction (GRT2) with the Gore Range Trail, 2.6 miles from the trailhead. Turn right toward Surprise Lake, which you reach in a further 0.2 mile. The lake, covered with water lilies, is quite scenic and is definitely worth a visit.

To reach Upper Cataract Lake, continue on the trail as it climbs steeply west to another trail junction at mile 3.3, where the Upper Cataract Trail leaves the Gore Range Trail (GRT3). Stay left at this junction and follow the trail southwest, reaching Upper Cataract Lake at mile 5.2. The small lake visible just before descending to Upper Cataract Lake is Cat Lake (or Kat Lake, according to the sign). The rugged peak behind Upper Cataract Lake is Eagles Nest.

ROUTE DESCRIPTION: To continue to Dora Lake, backtrack along the trail for 0.3 mile and look for a point at 10,900 feet where a ridge takes off to the south-southeast. A cairn may mark this point, and if you look carefully, you'll find a climbers' trail (GRT4) heading through the trees up this ridge. The ridge defines the top of the cliffs immediately east of Upper Cataract Lake.

Gary starting across the ridge. The initial scrambling is quite easy.

Follow the climbers' trail, occasionally marked with cairns, as it rises steeply for 1,700 feet before the grade relents on the plateau. You are now at the start of the long east ridge of Eagles Nest.

The ridge to the summit goes well, and you stay on the top of the ridge essentially the whole way. There is one tricky downclimb of a minor ridge point (GRT5), the third ridge point of the traverse. A series of ledges and ramps on the south side of the ridge provides a workable route. Take a break on the summit of Eagles Nest. You've earned it. However, there is still plenty of work remaining.

From Eagles Nest, head south down the ridge toward Mount Powell. The descent to the low point of the ridge is straightforward, and you should be able to stay on top of the ridge. From the low point on, things get much more complicated. When we climbed this route, we attempted half a dozen times to follow the crest of the ridge over a series of gendarmes, and each time, we were forced to either drop off the west side of the ridge or backtrack to a lower traverse. Much of this section of the ridge would be Class 5 if you stayed on top.

The crux section of the traverse over to Mount Powell, seen from Eagles Nest.

Looking back at Eagles Nest from Mount Powell.

You will save several hundred feet of elevation gain and loss by staying on the west side of the ridge for this section.

Eventually, the complex route finding ends on the broad summit plateau of Powell. From here, it is a simple walk over to the summit.

To descend from Powell, it is necessary to go down the "normal" route, the south gully, a tedious scree slope with many slippery social trails. (Note: When ascending this route from Kneeknocker Pass [the unofficial name for the pass between Mount Powell and Peak C], you'll find better rock if you stay on the ridge to the west of the gully. However, that ridge would be slow to descend.) Persevere with the gully and reach a point below Kneeknocker Pass. Choose one of several routes up and over the pass, eventually dropping into the basin north of Peak C's southwest ridge. Pick up the notorious trail that approximately (very approximately!) follows a minor drainage, and intersect the main trail at 9,715 feet (GRT6). Follow the main trail west as it stays on the north side of Piney River. Continue to the parking area west of Piney Lake. Collapse at the car.

30. Keller Mountain—East Ridge

Keller Mountain from the east. The route heads up the broad east ridge before traversing left to right in this photo.

ROUND-TRIP DISTANCE	9.85 miles
ROUND-TRIP TIME	8 hours
STARTING ELEVATION	9,470 feet
HIGHEST ELEVATION	13,085 feet
ELEVATION GAIN	4,045 feet
SEASON	June to October
JURISDICTION	White River National Forest, Dillon Ranger District, Eagles Nest Wilderness
MAP	Willow Lakes 7.5 minute

OVERVIEW: A trail approach to a moderate ridge run offering plenty of Class 3 scrambling.

GETTING THERE: From the Silverthorne exit on Interstate 70, head north on Colorado 9 for 7.7 miles. Turn left on the Rock Creek Road. After 1.3 miles, take the left fork, signed as Rock Creek Forest Service Access. Drive a further 1.6 miles on this rough road to the parking area. Four-wheel-drive vehicles are recommended.

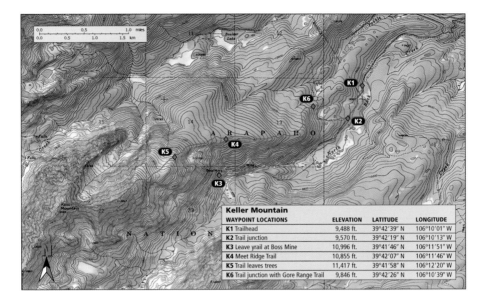

Keller Mountain			
WAYPOINT LOCATIONS	**ELEVATION**	**LATITUDE**	**LONGITUDE**
K1 Trailhead	9,488 ft.	39°42'39" N	106°10'01" W
K2 Trail junction	9,570 ft.	39°42'19" N	106°10'13" W
K3 Leave yrail at Boss Mine	10,996 ft.	39°41'46" N	106°11'51" W
K4 Meet Ridge Trail	10,855 ft.	39°42'07" N	106°11'46" W
K5 Trail leaves trees	11,417 ft.	39°41'58" N	106°12'20" W
K6 Trail junction with Gore Range Trail	9,846 ft.	39°42'26" N	106°10'39" W

COMMENT: An old favorite, Keller Mountain is one of those routes to which we keep returning. With moderate scrambling, it is also one of the best routes for an introduction to the sport.

Having said that, you can spice it up by extending the season and climbing this one on snow. In these conditions, the ridge is, of course, quite a bit more serious and will test the seasoned scrambler. On one occasion we

Climbing the grassy slopes up to the ridge.

Ginni gaining the start of the ridge proper.

were climbing this ridge in the late autumn. The route was snow-covered. Ginni slipped at an exposed spot on the ridge and fell over backward. Her helmet and a ledge several feet down saved her from injury, thank goodness. Don't take the route too lightly.

With that caveat, let me reiterate that the scrambling is delightful and provides a great outing in a stunning location.

APPROACH: The normal approach to Keller Mountain uses the hiking trail to the Boss Mine before heading up to the ridge. I think that a better route uses an abandoned trail off the Gore Range Trail. For completeness, I'll describe both routes, using the Boss Mine approach on the way up and descending via the abandoned trail.

ROUTE DESCRIPTION: From the parking area, start hiking up the Rock Creek Trail, initially very wide. The trail winds up the valley on the north side of North Rock Creek, passing the first mine at mile 1.7. Continue past this mine on the main trail to the Boss Mine (K3) after 2.2 miles. Look for a cairned trail taking off to the right. This trail wanders steeply uphill through the mine ruins (actually there are several confusing trails through this section—stay with one that heads generally uphill to the north) and eventually joins the ridge trail at mile 2.7 (K4). Turn left (west) and follow this trail along the ridge to tree line at mile 3.3 (K5). A cairn marks the place where

Keller Peak's summit ridge.

the trail exits the trees. Take careful note of this location for your return, since there are several trails above this point that are not well defined.

Continue up the ridge, using existing trails where possible. A variation cuts across a broad basin to the right (north) of the ridge. Both trails come together before reaching a ridge point at 12,847 feet (mile 4.3), the start of the scrambling. From the vantage point at 12,847 feet, the ridge to the summit is laid out in front of you. Several ridge points lie between you and your goal, which is still 0.8 mile away. The ridge is quite easy until you reach a prominent ridge point at 12,922 feet, one quarter of the way along the scramble. Dropping off the west end of this point requires a tricky downclimb, first down the crest, then dropping off to the left (south) side. Continue on, staying close to the ridge for some fun scrambling, until you reach a rounded ridge point that marks the end of the difficulties. Turn southwest and reach the summit on easy terrain.

Reverse your route until you reach K4, where we'll leave our track and continue down the ridge on a good abandoned trail. Stay on the main trail as it curves gently north (left), following the broad ridge crest; don't be tempted by a number of spur trails that drop steeply off to your right. The trail curves back to the east (right) before abruptly meeting the well-defined Gore Range Trail (K6). Turn right onto the Gore Range Trail and follow it as it winds around, first south then east, rejoining the Rock Creek Trail at K2. Turn left and head back to your vehicle.

Tenmile Range & Mosquito Range

The Mohawk Lakes.

Forming the southern end of the Park Range, these relatively small ranges are squeezed in between Colorado 9 on the east and Colorado 91 on the west. Access to the routes will be from one of these highways. The Tenmile Range starts south of Interstate 70 and becomes the Mosquito Range west of Hoosier Pass, extending south to Weston Pass.

These areas have a very different mining history than the Gore Range. This has resulted in many access roads and old mines. Expect to come across the remains of many abandoned mines.

The rock of the Tenmile Range traverse is highly fractured.

THE ROCK

I wish I could say that the rock in these ranges was really good. Unfortunately, that wouldn't be accurate. The complex geology of this area creates quite variable rock quality. While the rock on the north ridge of Quandary is some of the best, the ridge above Mayflower Gulch must be some of the worst. The rock along this ridge is granitic gneiss, hard but fractured. Although this area is not as heavily glaciated as its neighboring range to the north (the Gore Range), the effects of glaciation can still be readily seen.

31. Tenmile Range Traverse

The Tenmile Range traverse, from Tenmile Peak on the right to Peak 4 at left.

ROUND-TRIP DISTANCE	14 miles from Miners Creek Trailhead
ROUND-TRIP TIME	9 hours
STARTING ELEVATION	9,095 feet
HIGHEST ELEVATION	12,933 feet
ELEVATION GAIN	4,500 feet
SEASON	June to October
JURISDICTION	White River National Forest, Dillon Ranger District
MAP	Frisco 7.5 minute

OVERVIEW: A fun ridge with mainly Class 3 and some Class 4 scrambling.

GETTING THERE: From exit 203 off Interstate 70 at Frisco, drive south on Colorado 9 for 1.5 miles. Turn right (south) at the sign for County Commons (County Road 1004). Almost immediately, take a right, then a left, following the signs for Miners Creek. Park at the sign for the Miners Creek Trailhead (T1) in another 0.25 mile. The route can be shortened by

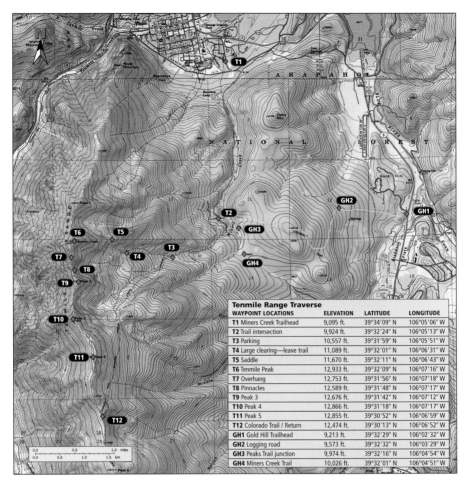

Tenmile Range Traverse			
WAYPOINT LOCATIONS	**ELEVATION**	**LATITUDE**	**LONGITUDE**
T1 Miners Creek Trailhead	9,095 ft.	39°34′09″ N	106°05′06″ W
T2 Trail intersection	9,924 ft.	39°32′24″ N	106°05′13″ W
T3 Parking	10,557 ft.	39°31′59″ N	106°05′51″ W
T4 Large clearing—leave trail	11,089 ft.	39°32′01″ N	106°06′31″ W
T5 Saddle	11,670 ft.	39°32′11″ N	106°06′43″ W
T6 Tenmile Peak	12,933 ft.	39°32′09″ N	106°07′16″ W
T7 Overhang	12,753 ft.	39°31′56″ N	106°07′18″ W
T8 Pinnacles	12,589 ft.	39°31′48″ N	106°07′17″ W
T9 Peak 3	12,676 ft.	39°31′42″ N	106°07′12″ W
T10 Peak 4	12,866 ft.	39°31′18″ N	106°07′17″ W
T11 Peak 5	12,855 ft.	39°30′52″ N	106°06′59″ W
T12 Colorado Trail / Return	12,474 ft.	39°30′13″ N	106°06′52″ W
GH1 Gold Hill Trailhead	9,213 ft.	39°32′29″ N	106°02′32″ W
GH2 Logging road	9,573 ft.	39°32′32″ N	106°03′29″ W
GH3 Peaks Trail junction	9,974 ft.	39°32′16″ N	106°04′54″ W
GH4 Miners Creek Trail	10,026 ft.	39°32′01″ N	106°04′51″ W

the use of a high-clearance four-wheel-drive vehicle. With this, it is possible to drive to the intersection with the Colorado Trail (T3), saving 3.2 miles each way and 1,400 feet of elevation gain. A partial barrier at the trailhead gives the appearance that you can't drive beyond the trailhead; but in actuality, you can pass between the two posts and drive up the paved, one-lane road for 0.25 mile, cross a bike path, then continue left up the two-lane dirt road. The road is too rough and rocky beyond the first mile or so for regular cars.

COMMENT: The Tenmile Range is the prominent line of peaks extending south from Interstate 70 to Breckenridge. While a complete traverse of the range is a fine objective, I have found that the best scrambling can be had

Approaching the first notch.

PHOTO BY TERRY ROOT

by climbing a subset of the peaks. The route described here has the advantage of returning you to the starting point. It also takes you up the very aesthetic east ridge of Tenmile Peak, rather than climbing the somewhat tedious north ridge of Peak 1 over Royal Mountain with its confusing mess of logging trails.

This route climbs Tenmile Peak (12,933 feet), Peak 3 (12,676 feet), Peak 4 (12,866 feet), and Peak 5 (12,855 feet).

APPROACH: Assuming that you'll have to hoof it, walk up the four-wheel-drive road for 3.2 miles to the junction with the Colorado Trail, passing the signed turnoff to Rainbow Lake after a half mile. There are many unsigned side roads in the last mile, some of which return back to the road. While the main stem of the road is marked with orange diamonds on the trees, these are too few and far between to be useful. Stay on what appears to be the main track, bearing right at a head-scratching intersection at about mile 2.5 (T2), the only intersection that appears on the topo. Beyond this,

most of the side roads rejoin
the main track, as the road
steepens considerably before
ending at a small parking
area and corral (T3).

After the second notch, climb up the left side of this feature to gain the ridge crest.

At this point, the
Colorado Trail meets the
Miners Creek Trail. Leave the
parking area and head west
on the combined trail, soon
crossing Miners Creek on a
corduroy bridge. Ascend
through the spruce forest,
veering sharply south into a
large clearing (T4). From
here, you have a wonderful
view in profile of the entire
sweep of ridge from Tenmile
Peak on your right to Peak 5
on the left. The east ridge of
Tenmile Peak is immediately
to your right, and this is where you leave the trail and gain the ridge. Work
your way up the ridge through trees and clearings to a saddle at T5.

ROUTE DESCRIPTION: Scramble west up the ridge. Above tree line, the ridge
becomes increasingly rocky and provides some nice Class 3 scrambling.
From the summit of Tenmile Peak (T6), head south. Almost immediately
downclimb into a notch and traverse around the west (right) side of a gendarme before regaining the ridge at the second notch.

Climb up the left side of the next obstacle and continue along the ridge
crest until you are stopped by an overhanging downclimb.

Backtrack perhaps 50 feet until you can downclimb 20 feet on the east
side of the ridge and bypass the overhang (T7).

The very next feature provides the route's crux—I call it "the Dragon."
Gain the ridge by climbing a narrow ledge/crack system on the Dragon's
"neck," and then balance along the very exposed ridge.

There is an interesting downclimb to exit the ridge from the Dragon's
"tail."

The Dragon is the crux of this traverse.

The last bit of exposed scrambling.

The fun ridge up Peak 4.

Climb one more exposed section of ridge before dropping off to the right (west) to avoid three small but difficult pinnacles (T8). Pass these pinnacles on a ledge and head over to the summit of Peak 3 (T9) on easy terrain.

The fun isn't quite over yet. Walk down the ridge to the saddle between Peak 3 and Peak 4. The ridge up to Peak 4 isn't difficult but provides very nice Class 3 scrambling on solid rock.

After reaching the top of Peak 4 (T10), continue on the now easy ridge walk over to Peak 5 (T11) and intersect the Miners Creek Trail (T12). Follow the trail back down until it rejoins your up track.

Note: An alternative approach starts at the Gold Hill Trailhead on Colorado 9. From the trailhead (GH1), hike west on the Gold Hill Trail (also the Colorado Trail). After 1 mile, meet a logging road (GH2). Go left on the trail. After 3 miles (GH3), join the Peaks Trail and turn left toward the Miners Creek Trail. At GH4, take the Miners Creek Trail to the right and follow it to T3, where the jeep road meets the trail.

This alternative route has a total elevation gain of 5,300 feet and a round-trip distance of 16.4 miles—for the energetic!

32. Quandary Peak—North Ridge

The route described ascends the rock slabs directly above the snowfield.

ROUND-TRIP DISTANCE	5.5 miles (plus 1 mile to connect trailheads)
ROUND-TRIP TIME	6 hours
STARTING ELEVATION	10,096 feet
HIGHEST ELEVATION	14,265 feet
ELEVATION GAIN	3,200 feet
SEASON	June to October
JURISDICTION	White River National Forest, Dillon Ranger District
MAP	Breckenridge 7.5 minute

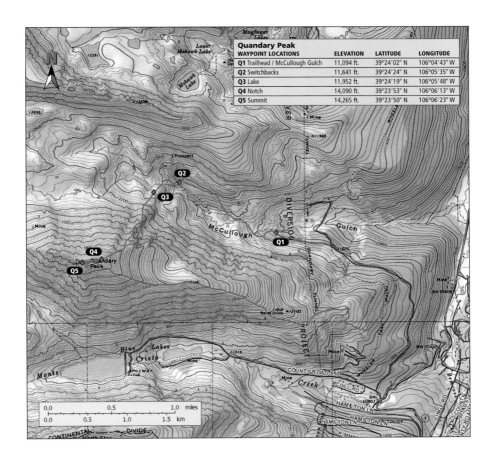

Quandary Peak			
WAYPOINT LOCATIONS	**ELEVATION**	**LATITUDE**	**LONGITUDE**
Q1 Trailhead / McCullough Gulch	11,094 ft.	39°24'02" N	106°04'43" W
Q2 Switchbacks	11,641 ft.	39°24'24" N	106°05'35" W
Q3 Lake	11,952 ft.	39°24'19" N	106°05'48" W
Q4 Notch	14,090 ft.	39°23'53" N	106°06'13" W
Q5 Summit	14,265 ft.	39°23'50" N	106°06'23" W

OVERVIEW: A fine route, with challenging scrambling on mostly solid rock. May involve short sections of lower Class 5 climbing.

GETTING THERE: From Colorado 9, 2.4 miles north of Hoosier Pass, turn onto Blue Lakes Road. After 0.1 mile, turn right (northeast) and follow this road for 2.1 miles to the McCullough Gulch Trailhead, staying left at the fork at 1.6 miles.

The route described starts up the slabs shown here.

COMMENT: Most people know Quandary as an easy "walk-up," possibly as a snow climb, or as a good ski-mountaineering objective. Quandary is often one of the first Fourteeners for people chasing that list.

Few know that hidden on the peak's north side is a delightful scramble with a very alpine feel, away from the crowds. As you ascend this route, enjoy good views of the east ridge of Pacific Peak, directly across the valley.

A few lower Class 5 moves may be encountered.

APPROACH: From the parking area in McCullough Gulch (Q1), head west up the trail for 1.25 miles to the lake (Q3) at the base of the north ridge. As you hike up the trail, you can see the objective on the skyline ahead of you. The route starts from the south side of the lake, between the prominent ridgeline to the left and the often snow-filled couloir to the right.

ROUTE DESCRIPTION: Cross the lake outlet if possible. When we did the climb, it was early enough in the season that the stream was quite high, so we elected to go around the west end of the lake to avoid having to wade.

Scramble south up scree and talus for a hundred feet. At this point, there are many options, so choose the one that looks best, heading generally for the obvious towers 500 feet above you. The climbing initially consists of sections of solid, low-angled, slabby

Fine scrambling near the start of the route.

rock, grassy ledges, and some sections of broken ground.

Judicious route finding keeps the difficulty at no more than easy Class 5 and provides very enjoyable scrambling. While we carried a rope and small rack (not knowing what to expect), we didn't break the gear out

Upper section of ridge.

for this section, although some parties might want the security of a rope. If so, be careful with your rope management, as there would be a significant chance of the rope bringing down rocks on members of your group.

As you approach the towers on the ridge, choose your line. Attacking the towers directly provides reasonable Class 4 passage, or continue along the right side of the towers on pleasant third-class terrain, consisting of solid rock and more grassy sections. Either way, you will hit the ridge above the towers in a few hundred feet. Follow the ridge as it trends slightly right, or stay immediately to its right side. Turn left at an obvious notch, drop down 20 feet, cross a small gully, and continue up. As usual, the rock on the ridge tends to be of better quality than that in the gullies. At an abrupt notch in the ridge (Q4), it is advisable to downclimb 30 feet to your right rather than jump across, as certain individuals have been known to do. Regain the ridge.

Shortly after this you will reach what appears to be a natural way to bypass a small tower to the left. This way takes you into a very loose gully composed of rotten, yellow rock that is difficult to escape from (one member of our group who took this line needed a belay to climb out). Instead, scramble up the small tower to the right.

Continue up on technically easier ground (but looser) until you gain the broad East Ridge at 13,800 feet. From here, it is an easy walk to the summit (Q5).

It is best to descend via the excellent trail along the gentle East Ridge to the Quandary Trailhead.

33. Pacific Peak—East Ridge

The east ridge of Pacific Peak, seen from high on Quandary Peak.

ROUND-TRIP DISTANCE	8 miles
ROUND-TRIP TIME	7 hours
STARTING ELEVATION	10,940 feet
HIGHEST ELEVATION	13,950 feet
ELEVATION GAIN	3,350 feet
SEASON	June to October
JURISDICTION	White River National Forest, Dillon Ranger District
MAP	Breckenridge 7.5 minute

OVERVIEW: Scramble up grassy slopes to ridgeline, then run the ridge over increasingly rocky terrain until you reach the plateau below Pacific Peak. From here, it is an easy scramble up the peak. Descend into McCullough Gulch and follow the trail and the road back to your vehicle.

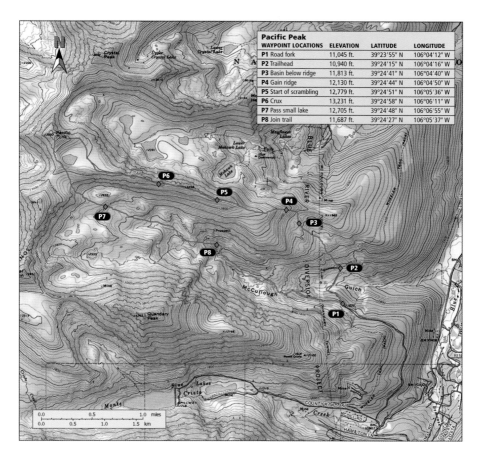

Pacific Peak			
WAYPOINT LOCATIONS	**ELEVATION**	**LATITUDE**	**LONGITUDE**
P1 Road fork	11,045 ft.	39°23'55" N	106°04'12" W
P2 Trailhead	10,940 ft.	39°24'15" N	106°04'16" W
P3 Basin below ridge	11,813 ft.	39°24'41" N	106°04'40" W
P4 Gain ridge	12,130 ft.	39°24'44" N	106°04'50" W
P5 Start of scrambling	12,779 ft.	39°24'51" N	106°05'36" W
P6 Crux	13,231 ft.	39°24'58" N	106°06'11" W
P7 Pass small lake	12,705 ft.	39°24'48" N	106°06'55" W
P8 Join trail	11,687 ft.	39°24'27" N	106°05'37" W

GETTING THERE: From Colorado 9, 2.4 miles north of Hoosier Pass, turn onto Blue Lakes Road. After 0.1 mile, turn right (northeast) and follow this road for 1.6 miles to a junction (P1). Take the right fork and continue for a further 0.6 mile to a small parking area on the north side of the road (P2). This parking spot is about 100 yards past the intersection with the Wheeler Trail.

COMMENT: This is a *fun* route. Just when you think it might be a "walk in the park," the ridge becomes interesting and varied and remains so for quite awhile. It even has a knife-edge.

APPROACH: From the parking area, head up gentle, grassy slopes northwest, toward a basin that provides access to the ridge (P3). Continue up to the ridge.

ROUTE DESCRIPTION: Once you are on the ridge (P4), turn west and follow the top of the ridge over easy terrain, which gradually becomes more interesting as several ridge points are passed. In general, all ridge points can be climbed directly.

Start of the Class 3 scrambling.

The ridge turns out to be much longer than expected, with lots of moderate climbing. For me, the high point of the ridge was the knife-edge: airy climbing on reasonable rock (P6).

After negotiating the knife-edge, half an hour of further scrambling brings you to the broad plateau under Pacific's summit block.

From here, it is a simple walk up to the summit by one of the ridges.

A reasonable descent route takes you down into McCullough Gulch, heading just south of the lake at 12,695 feet. Pick up the McCullough Gulch Trail below Quandary's north ridge, on the north side of the unnamed lake (P8).

Follow the good trail to the McCullough Gulch Trailhead. Walk down the dirt road to the point where the road forks (P1). Turn left (north) and follow the road back to your vehicle.

Looking back at the fine knife-edge.

34. Father Dyer Peak

Approaching Father Dyer's surprising summit.

ROUND-TRIP DISTANCE	7.5 miles
ROUND-TRIP TIME	5 hours
STARTING ELEVATION	10,975 feet
HIGHEST ELEVATION	13,852 feet
ELEVATION GAIN	3,000 feet
SEASON	Late May to October
JURISDICTION	White River National Forest, Dillon Ranger District
MAP	Breckenridge 7.5 minute

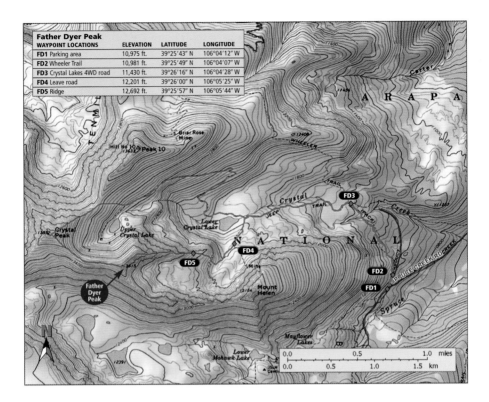

Father Dyer Peak WAYPOINT LOCATIONS	ELEVATION	LATITUDE	LONGITUDE
FD1 Parking area	10,975 ft.	39°25'43" N	106°04'12" W
FD2 Wheeler Trail	10,981 ft.	39°25'49" N	106°04'07" W
FD3 Crystal Lakes 4WD road	11,430 ft.	39°26'16" N	106°04'28" W
FD4 Leave road	12,201 ft.	39°26'00" N	106°05'25" W
FD5 Ridge	12,692 ft.	39°25'57" N	106°05'44" W

OVERVIEW: A hike along a good trail and jeep roads with moderate and enjoyable Class 3 scrambling on an exposed ridge.

GETTING THERE: From the Boreas Pass Road junction at the south end of Breckenridge (the last traffic light as you leave town), follow Colorado 9 for 2.1 miles south to Spruce Creek Road. Head southwest and west for 2.4 miles (being careful to stay on Spruce Creek Road) to a parking area at a sharp right-hand turn. The four-wheel-drive road continuing straight at this point goes to the Mohawk Lakes. Passenger cars may need to park about a mile before this point at the winter trailhead. A rough branch road taking off to the right, shortly after the winter parking area, is not recommended for driving, although if you have parked lower down it can save some hiking time.

COMMENT: While not a ranked peak (just a sub-peak of Crystal Peak—13,852 feet), the east ridge of Father Dyer presents an aesthetic and enjoyable scramble.

Approaching Father Dyer Peak. Lower Crystal Lake is in the foreground. Crystal Peak can just be seen at the far right.

This route provides a good introduction to the "art" of scrambling, offering some exposed but not sustained climbing and even a bit of loose rock to initiate the budding scrambler.

Because of the relatively short (less than 1,000 feet) ridge being climbed, the commitment level is lower than many of the other routes described in this guide, although as Ginni and I discovered one June morning, the rapid buildup of thunderclouds can still necessitate a hurried descent.

After jumping on a series of snowfields to bail off the ridge between Father Dyer and Crystal, we arrived back at Lower Crystal Lake. As we were putting our ice axes away, a nearby hiker commented that we had all the gear with us, including our "whackers" (ice axes?). As on many other occasions, we were happy to have had our "whackers" along.

APPROACH: From the parking area (FD1), hike north up the access road for Francie's Cabin. Shortly after passing a closed gate, turn left onto the Wheeler Trail (FD2) and follow this for 0.6 mile, where you will meet the Crystal Lakes four-wheel-drive road (FD3). Take the four-wheel-drive road west for 0.9 mile until it makes a sharp left turn (FD4).

Ginni on the ridge with Lower Crystal Lake below.

ROUTE DESCRIPTION:
Leave the four-wheel-drive road here and head up a shallow drainage to the left of the ridge into the basin between Father Dyer and Mount Helen until you can make an easy ascending traverse on grassy slopes up to the ridge (FD5).

Scramble up the ridge, staying on the crest. Short sections of the ridge become narrow and exposed, but the difficulty never exceeds Class 3. One section has some loose rock and requires testing all holds, but this part is quite short.

Continue up the ridge and hike over to the surprisingly small summit block.

The best descent route goes over Crystal Peak to the saddle between Crystal and Peak 10. From here, drop down to the jeep trail near Upper Crystal Lake and follow this down to the lower lake where you rejoin your up track.

The difficulty never exceeds class 3.

35. Mayflower Gulch Grand Traverse

A section of Rockfountain Ridge, showing Fletcher Mountain at the left (photo taken from McCullough Gulch).

ROUND-TRIP DISTANCE	7.3 miles
ROUND-TRIP TIME	12 hours
STARTING ELEVATION	11,541 feet
HIGHEST ELEVATION	13,951 feet
ELEVATION GAIN	3,800 feet
SEASON	June to September
JURISDICTION	White River National Forest, Dillon Ranger District
MAP	Copper Mountain 7.5 minute

OVERVIEW: A difficult climb with more than one dangerously loose section. A rope is a requirement on this scramble. This is arguably the most dangerous route in this guidebook.

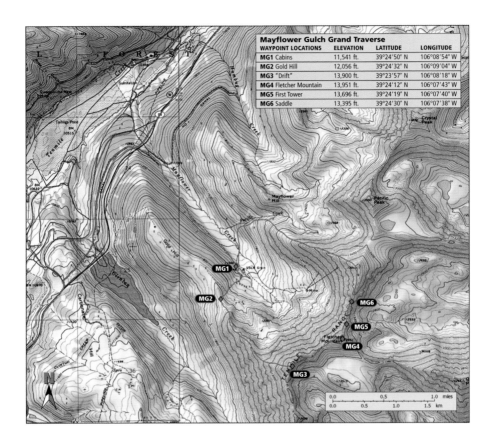

Mayflower Gulch Grand Traverse			
WAYPOINT LOCATIONS	ELEVATION	LATITUDE	LONGITUDE
MG1 Cabins	11,541 ft.	39°24′50″ N	106°08′54″ W
MG2 Gold Hill	12,056 ft.	39°24′32″ N	106°09′04″ W
MG3 "Drift"	13,900 ft.	39°23′57″ N	106°08′18″ W
MG4 Fletcher Mountain	13,951 ft.	39°24′12″ N	106°07′43″ W
MG5 First Tower	13,696 ft.	39°24′19″ N	106°07′40″ W
MG6 Saddle	13,395 ft.	39°24′30″ N	106°07′38″ W

GETTING THERE: From exit 195 on Interstate 70 (Copper Mountain), take Colorado 91 south for 6.1 miles to the Mayflower Gulch turnoff.

COMMENT: This scramble offers a circumnavigation of the peaks and ridges ringing Mayflower Gulch. This seldom-climbed, rugged ridge offers some challenging route finding. An impressive series of both major and minor towers spouting up in the final third of the traverse has inspired local climbers to dub this "Rockfountain Ridge."

The route can be climbed in either direction; however, the traverse from Unnamed 13,841 ("Atlantic Peak") to Fletcher Mountain (13,951 feet) involves two pitches of technical climbing up to 5.7 in difficulty, with some loose blocks the size of refrigerators. If climbed in the opposite direction, these pitches can be rappelled.

When Ginni and I climbed the route from "Atlantic" to "Drift," we used rock shoes for the two technical pitches mentioned above. Starting up the ridge, the climbing appeared to be no more than Class 4. Thirty feet up the ridge, however, the blocks started to move with the least touch, so I was forced to traverse right to more solid ground. A 20-foot, 5.7 finger crack provided a workable route. After this, the terrain became easier, but we had to take extreme care that the rope didn't dislodge any of the loose blocks above. A second, easier pitch took us to the end of the technical difficulties.

The route will be described from "Drift Peak" to "Atlantic." Bring at least a 50-meter (165-foot) rope to rappel the technical sections, as well as to raise the comfort level on the extensive (not to mention very loose) Class 4 terrain.

APPROACH: Hike or drive up the four-wheel-drive road into Mayflower Gulch for 1.5 miles (MG1) to some cabins. Actually, any vehicle with good clearance can normally make it to tree line. From here, take mining roads southwest, climbing toward a low spot on the ridge labeled "Gold Hill" on topos (MG2). Turn generally south and boulder hop steeply up the ridge to the point at 13,900 feet (MG3). I've always called this "Gold Hill," but more recently the name "Drift Peak" has been adopted by most mountaineers.

ROUTE DESCRIPTION: The 0.6 mile on the ridge northeast to Fletcher Mountain provides very moderate scrambling, except for a short upclimb from the low point. This 30-foot step is at least Class 4, and many parties will prefer to use a rope (if climbing in the opposite direction, it is best to rappel this step). From the low point, move left and climb up the loose gully, exiting just over the left shoulder of the step. There is a short, exposed downclimb on delicately poised talus before squeezing behind a prominent flake to easy ground.

From the top of Fletcher (MG4), continue north along the ridge to "Atlantic." Shortly after leaving the summit of Fletcher, you will come to the technical step described in the Comment. Two rappels are required to pass the first of the major towers (MG5). There are five major gendarmes and a handful of minor towers to be negotiated before reaching "Atlantic," but all can be climbed or bypassed on Class 3 and 4 terrain, although complex route finding makes this section very slow to negotiate. With one exception, the rock quality of these towers is often poor, compounding the difficulties.

After rappelling into the notch at the base of the first tower, scramble up the second major tower, passing several feet left of its summit. Descend on Class 3 terrain to a notch on the far side of the tower and then begin an

Scramblers along the ridge between "Drift" and Fletcher.   PHOTO BY TERRY ROOT

enjoyable romp over the tops of four minor points in the next 50 yards. You'll find yourself straddling this exposed knife-edge with occasional detours to the left around individual blocks.

Arriving at the cut just below the third major tower, traverse left for 15 feet and then scamper straight up a steep, shallow trough that crests to the left of the tower's summit block. Despite exposure, the rock here is sound compared to the uncertain holds and loose blocks looming overhead on much of this ridge. Pass over the left shoulder and carefully pick a way down for 50 feet. You will come to an intermediate dip, where another rappel is required to reach the notch between the third and fourth towers. You can avoid the rappel by downclimbing to the left, following a gully that descends toward Mayflower Gulch. The gully itself is too loose for comfort, so stay on the rib that forms the right-hand side. Descend this for 150 feet and locate a narrow, snaking couloir that descends to your right. Pick your way down this as it first parallels the rib, then turns back to the right, dumping you out into the gully between the third and fourth towers.

Trudge back up the scree of this gully, toward the "V" notch (the lowest point of the entire ridge), and traverse left onto the rotten slopes of the fourth tower, aiming again to pass over just left of its top. Although you can pick your way with care down for 40 feet on steep, blocky steps along the crest, you may choose to rappel again or set up a hand line. Once you are into the saddle between the fourth and fifth major towers (MG6), breathe a little easier, because

Scrambling over the shoulder near the summit of the second tower.
PHOTO BY TERRY ROOT

major difficulties are at an end. (And if bad weather or fatigue is setting in, the gully descending from this saddle offers an easy escape down to Mayflower Gulch.) The final gendarme, and the remaining 450 feet up to "Atlantic," involve mostly boulder hopping, passing minor obstacles on their right.

From the top of "Atlantic," descend the narrow but easy west ridge until it is possible to drop into the Mayflower Gulch drainage, staying just south of Pacific Creek. Cross the willows protecting Mayflower Creek and rejoin the trail for the last mile and a half back to the trailhead.

The Sawatch Range

La Plata's Ellingwood Ridge is one of the premier scrambles in the Sawatch.

The Sawatch Range is Colorado's "backbone," stretching from I-70 south to U.S. 50, west of U.S. 24.

Normally thought of as a range of gentle giants, there are some good scrambles hidden among the rounded summits. I've included three of the best.

History

The Ellingwood Ridge on La Plata Peak was first climbed by none other than Albert Ellingwood, in 1921—solo. Ellingwood was the climber who pushed technical climbing to a new level in Colorado's mountains during the 1910s to 1920s, with first ascents of such classics as Lizard Head and the Ellingwood Arete on Crestone Needle.

Ice Mountain wasn't climbed until 1931 by John L.J. Hart, who soloed the final summit ridge described in this guide (*Trail and Timberline*, Number 157, November 1931).

Some of the best rock in the Sawatch is found in the Holy Cross Wilderness, shown here on Fool's Peak.

THE ROCK

Most of the rock in the northern part of the Sawatch is composed of Precambrian gneiss and schist, hard but fractured.

36. Ellingwood Ridge

The famous Ellingwood Ridge.

ROUND-TRIP DISTANCE	9.6 miles
ROUND-TRIP TIME	9 to 12 hours
STARTING ELEVATION	10,190 feet
HIGHEST ELEVATION	14,336 feet
ELEVATION GAIN	4,900 feet
SEASON	Late June to October
JURISDICTION	San Isabel National Forest, Leadville Ranger District
MAPS	Independence Pass 7.5 minute; Mount Elbert 7.5 minute

OVERVIEW: A long and committing ridge run with opportunities for lots of Class 4 scrambling.

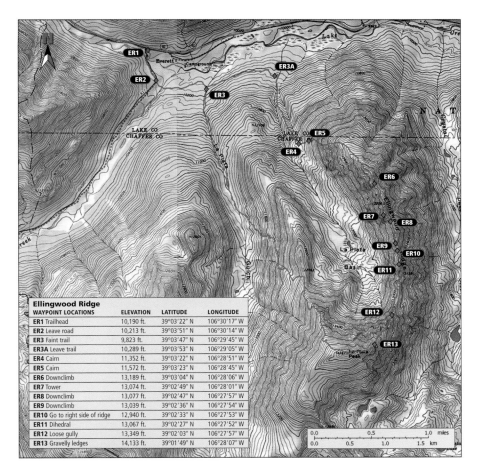

Ellingwood Ridge WAYPOINT LOCATIONS	ELEVATION	LATITUDE	LONGITUDE
ER1 Trailhead	10,190 ft.	39°03'22" N	106°30'17" W
ER2 Leave road	10,213 ft.	39°03'51" N	106°30'14" W
ER3 Faint trail	9,823 ft.	39°03'47" N	106°29'45" W
ER3A Leave trail	10,289 ft.	39°03'53" N	106°29'05" W
ER4 Cairn	11,352 ft.	39°03'22" N	106°28'51" W
ER5 Cairn	11,572 ft.	39°03'23" N	106°28'45" W
ER6 Downclimb	13,189 ft.	39°03'04" N	106°28'06" W
ER7 Tower	13,074 ft.	39°02'49" N	106°28'01" W
ER8 Downclimb	13,077 ft.	39°02'47" N	106°27'57" W
ER9 Downclimb	13,039 ft.	39°02'36" N	106°27'54" W
ER10 Go to right side of ridge	12,940 ft.	39°02'33" N	106°27'53" W
ER11 Dihedral	13,067 ft.	39°02'27" N	106°27'52" W
ER12 Loose gully	13,349 ft.	39°02'03" N	106°27'57" W
ER13 Gravelly ledges	14,133 ft.	39°01'49" N	106°28'07" W

GETTING THERE: From the intersection of U.S. 24 and Colorado 82, drive 14.5 miles west on Colorado 82 to a parking area adjacent to the South Fork Lake Creek Road. There is no parking along the South Fork Lake Creek Road.

COMMENT: The Ellingwood Ridge is one of the classic routes pioneered by the famous climber Albert Ellingwood. This is another committing route, and it should be attempted only in good weather. Once you have engaged the major difficulties of the ridge, retreat is not easy. Many parties race for the summit as afternoon thunderstorms roll in. Expect to spend at least five hours actually on the ridge.

You may notice that I've included more detail in this description than in most of the other routes in this book. This indicates the level of route-

finding complexity to keep the difficulty at no more than Class 4 while
enjoying the wonderful scrambling
that the ridge provides.

APPROACH: From the trailhead
(ER1), walk up the South Fork Road
for 0.2 mile across the bridge and up
to the point where the trail leaves
the road on the left (ER2). Follow
the excellent trail as it crosses first
the South Fork of Lake Creek on a
good bridge, then the stream in La
Plata Gulch on logs. Immediately
after crossing La Plata Gulch, the
main trail turns south to go up the
gulch. Follow this along the creek

The first difficulty—downclimbing the gendarme at waypoint ER6.

for 100 yards to a cairn marking a faint trail on your left (ER3). There are
other faint trails that take off between the stream crossing and this trail that
head in the same direction, but the trail marked by ER3 is the easiest to fol-

low, especially when starting out before sunrise. Take
this trail as it contours east
toward La Plata Basin. If
you're lucky, you may see a
northern goshawk in this
area of dense woods.

ROUTE DESCRIPTION: At
ER3A, the main branch of
the trail heads south up La
Plata Basin. You can take
this trail as it stays on the

Tower at waypoint ER7.

west side of the creek, but it becomes extremely rough because of downed
timber. It is better to continue east and cross the stream in less than 0.1
mile, heading for a small ridge immediately on the east side of the stream.
Turn south and pick up a trail, faint at first, which stays initially west of the
ridge crest but eventually joins the narrow crest. Follow the trail until it

Downclimbing one of the cruxes at waypoint ER8.

dies out at tree line, then pick a line up the tedious talus and scree slope, aiming for a point at the northern end of the Ellingwood Ridge. Cairns will be found as you ascend toward the ridge (ER4, ER5).

Pick your way through the cliff band. (Each time we've done this route, we've gone a different way and found none to be any better than another.) At about 12,600 feet, you are ready to start the infamous Ellingwood Ridge.

The goal is to stay on or close to the ridge crest the whole way. There is almost always a Class 4 or easier way to bypass or downclimb a difficult section, and there is never a need to descend more than 50 feet or so below the ridge, although your route-finding skills will be tested to accomplish this.

In a couple of spots, a climbers' trail will take you to the right (west) side of the ridge, but in general you will find yourself on or slightly left (east) of the crest.

Downclimbing at waypoint ER9.

The dihedral directly behind the second climber provides some of the more difficult moves on the route (ER11).

At ER6, drop a little way off the left (east) side of the ridge to avoid a cliff.

At ER7, climb over the tower shown on page 208. Downclimb it on the left side of the ridge.

The next crux requires some tricky downclimbing once again (ER8).

Intricate route finding and good rock keep your interest as you work your

The escape ledge, with patches of snow remaining, can be seen at lower left in this photo of Point 13,158.

way along the seemingly endless ridge. At ER9, there is another steep downclimb, as shown on page 209.

At ER10, the route goes well on the right side of the ridge.

Don't worry. One more difficult section (ER11) and the major difficulties are over, although you still have quite a way to go.

View from the saddle at Point 13,158. The loose gully at waypoint ER12 is shown in red.

The last obstacle before turning the corner is Point 13,158. Its face presents Class 5 climbing for sure, but luckily, a convenient ledge runs to the left across the face. This is your escape route and prevents you from having to lose considerable elevation to bypass this feature. The ledge takes you to a small saddle. From here, the rest of the route can be studied.

The next part of the route goes well along the ridge crest. At ER12, head for the loose gully to the left of the ridge and scramble up to the left ridgeline, passing a large chockstone by climbing the face to the left.

Climber working his way up to the chockstone.

After the chockstone, regain the ridge, scrambling up the large talus field and continuing until a smooth rock face is encountered at ER13. Contour

left on gravelly ledges to the ridgeline, and continue up easy terrain to the true summit.

As you descend down the standard trail on La Plata's northwest ridge, look over to your right and admire the route you just completed.

Contour left on the gravelly ledges to bypass the tower at ER13.

37. Ice Mountain—North Ridge

Ice Mountain with a fresh coat of snow.

ROUND-TRIP DISTANCE	8 miles
ROUND-TRIP TIME	8 to 9 hours
STARTING ELEVATION	10,636 feet
HIGHEST ELEVATION	13,951 feet
ELEVATION GAIN	3,300 feet
SEASON	June through October
JURISDICTION	San Isabel National Forest, Leadville Ranger District, Collegiate Peaks Wilderness
MAP	Winfield 7.5 minute

OVERVIEW: Trail and off-trail hiking to a saddle, followed by Class 3 scrambling along a ridge and a steep, short fourth-class finish.

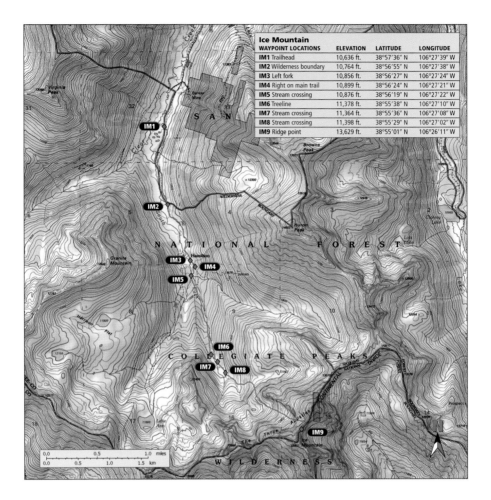

Ice Mountain			
WAYPOINT LOCATIONS	ELEVATION	LATITUDE	LONGITUDE
IM1 Trailhead	10,636 ft.	38°57′36″ N	106°27′39″ W
IM2 Wilderness boundary	10,764 ft.	38°56′55″ N	106°27′38″ W
IM3 Left fork	10,856 ft.	38°56′27″ N	106°27′24″ W
IM4 Right on main trail	10,899 ft.	38°56′24″ N	106°27′21″ W
IM5 Stream crossing	10,876 ft.	38°56′19″ N	106°27′22″ W
IM6 Treeline	11,378 ft.	38°55′38″ N	106°27′10″ W
IM7 Stream crossing	11,364 ft.	38°55′36″ N	106°27′08″ W
IM8 Stream crossing	11,398 ft.	38°55′29″ N	106°27′02″ W
IM9 Ridge point	13,629 ft.	38°55′01″ N	106°26′11″ W

GETTING THERE: Go 18.5 miles south of Leadville or 15 miles north of Buena Vista on U.S. 24, then turn west on County Road 390 and drive 11.7 miles to the old ghost town of Winfield. Turn left on County Road 290B in the center of Winfield, and drive 0.4 mile to a two-wheel-drive parking area. Park here, or shorten the climb by driving 1.8 miles further to the trailhead (IM1) along the four-wheel-drive road. A gate marks the end of the road. Two trails start by the gate—the left going to Huron and the one you want going straight (marked as the Colorado Trail).

COMMENT: We made a couple of attempts before summiting Ice Mountain. On one early-season trip, we postholed all the way up the South Fork of Clear Creek (what, snowshoes?—a bad decision had us leaving them at the

The route stays to the left of the cliff band as it gains the shoulder on North Apostle's northwest ridge.

car). Our original plan was to climb the fine snow couloir on Ice Mountain's north face, but snow conditions were not stable enough by the time we arrived at the base of the couloir, so we elected to try the ridge instead. After almost falling through the heavily corniced north ridge a couple of times, we turned around.

APPROACH: From the trailhead, follow the good trail to Apostle Basin. The trail crosses the Wilderness boundary after 0.85 mile (IM2).

At mile 1.5 (IM3) take the left trail fork to Apostle Basin. Stay right on the main trail at mile 1.6 (IM4). The left fork heads up an old mine road (and, as indicated on a tree, Huron.)

Follow the good trail south as it crosses a stream on a large log at mile 1.7 (IM5) and stays above and right of the stream draining Apostle Basin. The trail emerges into the basin at mile 2.5 (IM6). Follow the trail as it crosses a stream at mile 2.7 (IM7) before becoming less distinct in a marshy area. The trail crosses a stream again at mile 2.8 (IM8), then heads

Head for the gap on the left and then to the saddle between North Apostle and Ice Mountain.

to the toe of the obvious rock glacier. Follow a cairned trail around the left edge of the rock glacier and up a talus-strewn gully on its left side.

After leaving this gully, a cairned trail heads left up grassy slopes to reach a bench on the shoulder of North Apostle's northwest ridge. This avoids the cliffs barring access to the upper basin. Stay left of the willows as you head up to the bench.

ROUTE DESCRIPTION: Once on the shoulder, contour into the upper basin on climbers' trails, staying well left of the slabs in the middle of the valley. Aim for the notch, and head up to the saddle.

From the saddle, turn right and head up the ridge, climbing over and then descending one ridge point (IM9) and scrambling up on Class 3 terrain until it is necessary to cross a small, loose (and often snowy or icy) gully just before the summit. Cross to the right side of this gully (sometimes requiring a rope) and climb up to the ridge on steep, slabby rock, then continue along the ridge to the summit.

Descend by reversing the route.

View of summit ridge from IM9—the top of the crux gully can be seen just left of the summit.

38. Fools Peak—North Ridge

The north ridge of Fools Peak. The prominent notch is avoided by a spiralling ramp, out of sight in this view.

ROUND-TRIP DISTANCE	11.9 miles
ROUND-TRIP TIME	9 hours
STARTING ELEVATION	9,482 feet
HIGHEST ELEVATION	12,947 feet
ELEVATION GAIN	3,820 feet
SEASON	July through September
JURISDICTION	White River National Forest, Eagle–Holy Cross Ranger District
MAP	Mount Jackson 7.5 minute; Crooked Creek Pass 7.5 minute

OVERVIEW: A trail approach to great Class 3 and 4 scrambling on a solid quartzite ridge.

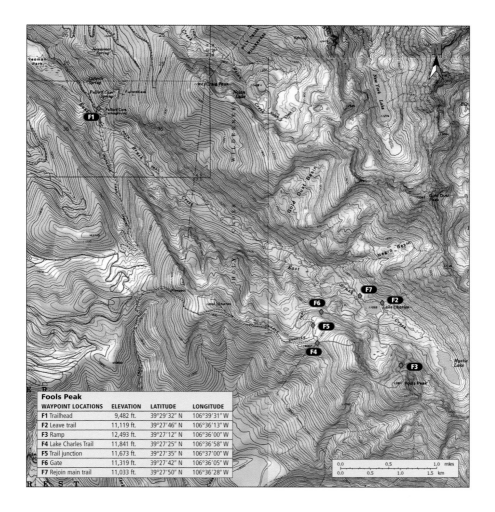

Fools Peak			
WAYPOINT LOCATIONS	ELEVATION	LATITUDE	LONGITUDE
F1 Trailhead	9,482 ft.	39°29'32" N	106°39'31" W
F2 Leave trail	11,119 ft.	39°27'46" N	106°36'13" W
F3 Ramp	12,493 ft.	39°27'12" N	106°36'00" W
F4 Lake Charles Trail	11,841 ft.	39°27'25" N	106°36'58" W
F5 Trail junction	11,673 ft.	39°27'35" N	106°37'00" W
F6 Gate	11,319 ft.	39°27'42" N	106°36'05" W
F7 Rejoin main trail	11,033 ft.	39°27'50" N	106°36'28" W

GETTING THERE: From Interstate 70, take exit 147 (Eagle) and head south, crossing the river bridge. Turn right on Grand Avenue (old Colorado 6) and drive to Capitol Street (the first street past the roundabout). Turn left and drive 0.8 mile before turning southeast (left) onto Brush Creek Road. Follow Brush Creek Road from its intersection with Capitol Street for 9.7 miles to a "Y" junction. Turn left onto East Brush Creek Road and take this road for a further 7.2 miles to the Fulford Cave Trailhead, immediately left of the Fulford Cave Campground. Note that after 5.8 miles on the East Brush Creek Road you will come to the Yeoman Park Campground. Stay straight here as the road narrows, and stay straight 0.4 mile further where a road takes off to the left. The road should be passable by passenger cars.

Detail of the lower ridge.

COMMENT: While climbing the east ridge of Gold Dust Peak, we noticed a stunning line on the peak across the valley. I determined to check it out, and a few weeks later I returned with a friend to climb it. The ridge exceeded our expectations, offering sustained third-class scrambling on excellent quartzite rock. The north ridge of Fools Peak didn't show signs of previous passage, so I even coined a name for the route, "No Fool Like an Old Fool," only to discover later that the route had indeed been climbed previously. Oh well.

APPROACH: After registering at the trailhead, hike through the gate and almost immediately look for a signed trail junction. The left fork heads to Lake Charles, and that's the way to go. The trail has been re-routed recently and no longer crosses Brush Creek, as shown on the map. In fact, the U.S. Forest Service is removing the logs spanning the creek.

The trail to Lake Charles gains 1,800 feet in 3.9 miles. Expect to spend at least two hours walking up this section of the trail, since its many twists and turns will slow you down a little. You will keep expecting to see the lake, only to find another hill to climb. When you do finally reach Lake Charles, however, you will be rewarded with very nice views of the lake and of Fools Peak beyond.

ROUTE DESCRIPTION:
Continue to the east end of Lake Charles (F2), then leave the trail and contour south around the lake, aiming for a prominent grassy gully that provides access to the basin northwest of the peak. Head up the gully into the basin. At tree line, contour east to gain the north ridge at 11,850 feet, possibly by a ramp system that cuts across the ridge.

Great scrambling on the solid quartzite.

The spiralling ramp used to access the notch.

The headwall, seen from the notch.

The scrambling is delightful, never exceeding Class 3 as you climb up and over minor ridge points. At 12,450 feet, the ridge changes, steepening to a point before a prominent notch. Descending into the notch would require one or more rappels. It is worth scrambling up to the top of this spire for the view, but to keep the difficulty at third class, look for a ramp (F3) which spirals around this ridge point to the right and deposits you at the base of the final headwall—600 feet of some of the best-quality rock you'll find in our mountains. With careful route finding, you should be able to keep the scrambling at Class 3 again, although there are plenty of options for some nice Class 4 scrambling. Work your way up this wall to the summit.

The descent route uses the standard route down to the Lake Charles Trail. From the summit, go west down the broad talus and scree slopes to the saddle at the head of the northwest basin. Dropping into this basin and rejoining your ascent route is a reasonable option, especially if the weather is threatening, but we chose to continue northwest along the ridge to a minor ridge point at 12,315 feet, then dropped west down to a saddle at 11,800 feet, where we picked up the Lake Charles Trail (F4). Follow the cairned trail as it drops back into the Brush Creek drainage. Note that the trail makes a long reach to the east, not shown on the topo map, below a cliff band, before dropping down to Lake Charles. Contour northwest around the lake and find a place to cross the outlet. Head northeast and rejoin the main trail in 100 yards (F7). Head back to the trailhead on the trail that now seems endless.

Climbing the headwall.

Indian Peaks Wilderness

The Indian Peaks reflected in Brainard Lake.

A southern extension of Rocky Mountain National Park, this area offers the same stunning scenery and great scrambling as its more famous neighbor.

Routes described in this guide use two approaches. The wild and remote area on the west side is accessed via the town of Granby, while the heavily used east-side routes are accessed via the Brainard Lake Trailhead.

In general, the west-side routes require a backpack, while most east-side routes can be climbed in a day from the trailhead. National Forest campgrounds are scattered along the Peak-to-Peak Highway (Colorado 72). An excellent campground is also available close to Brainard Lake, but this fills up quickly, especially on weekends. Some sites can be reserved. Permits are required for backcountry camping.

The granite of Lone Eagle Peak.

THE ROCK

This area features the same bomber granite (a climbing expression referring to the solidity of the rock) as that found to the north in Rocky Mountain National Park.

39. South Arapaho to North Arapaho Traverse

North Arapaho Peak, seen from the vicinity of the South Peak.

ROUND-TRIP DISTANCE	8.3 miles
ROUND-TRIP TIME	6 to 7 hours
STARTING ELEVATION	10,172 feet
HIGHEST ELEVATION	13,502 feet
ELEVATION GAIN	3,500 feet
SEASON	June to October
JURISDICTION	Roosevelt National Forest, Boulder Ranger District, Indian Peaks Wilderness
MAPS	Monarch Lake 7.5 minute; East Portal 7.5 minute

OVERVIEW: An easy trail hike and scramble to the summit of South Arapaho Peak, followed by a fun scramble to the north summit with some Class 3 and 4 terrain.

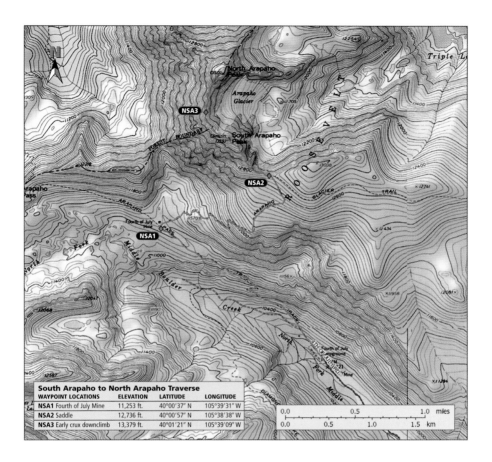

South Arapaho to North Arapaho Traverse			
WAYPOINT LOCATIONS	ELEVATION	LATITUDE	LONGITUDE
NSA1 Fourth of July Mine	11,253 ft.	40°00′37″ N	105°39′31″ W
NSA2 Saddle	12,736 ft.	40°00′57″ N	105°38′38″ W
NSA3 Early crux downclimb	13,379 ft.	40°01′21″ N	105°39′09″ W

GETTING THERE: From Nederland (west of Boulder on Colorado 119), drive west on Colorado 119 to the Eldora junction at the edge of town. Turn right here and head west, staying straight after 1.4 miles where the road to the Eldora Ski Area takes off to the left. At 4 miles, the road turns to dirt (shortly after passing through the town of Eldora). Continue to the Buckingham Campground (shown on the map as the Fourth of July Campground) at 8.8 miles. Trailhead parking is just uphill from the camp-ground.

COMMENT: This relatively short climb provides a good introduction to ridge scrambling. Additionally, spectacular views of the Indian Peaks Wilderness reward the climber.

When I led this trip for the Colorado Mountain Club many years ago, my "friend" and co-leader Charlie Winger decided to make the climb a

Orange arrows and cairns mark the climbers' trail.

little more challenging for me by adding a several-pound rock to my pack. Members of the trip (who saw this occur) expected Charlie to 'fess up at some point and were surprised when this didn't happen. I eventually discovered the "gift" on the way down. With friends like that...

By the way, the marmots are friendly. Please don't feed them.

Note: This climb is in the Indian Peaks Wilderness Area. Use is tightly regulated, so know the rules.

APPROACH: Hike up the Arapaho Pass Trail for 1.8 miles to the Fourth of July Mine (NSA1).

ROUTE DESCRIPTION: Take the right fork (Arapaho Glacier Trail) for 1.4 miles to the 12,736-foot low point on the ridge (NSA2) between South

An early crux.

Arapaho Peak and an unnamed point at 13,038 with great views of the Arapaho Glacier. From here, follow the southeast ridge of South Arapaho for 0.5 mile to its summit.

The scramble over to the north summit (0.7 mile)

is quite worthwhile. Follow the ridge on a climbers' trail (marked in places by orange paint).

Occasionally, the climbers' trail drops left (west) off the ridge. On most of these occasions it is possible to stay on or only slightly left of the ridge crest for more aesthetic climbing (I hate losing altitude!). The crux of this route is a short downclimb (Class 4), which some parties rappel. If you do use a rope here, you may want to leave it in place for the return trip.

The crux downclimb.

If you downclimb this section, it goes well to descend toward the climbers' left (facing out) into a shallow corner before descending right on ledges. By the way, a series of cairns do provide a way to bypass this step; however, it doesn't seem to be worth it.

As you approach the summit block, cairns lead left of the ridge into and up a gully. Cross into a second gully on the right and continue up this to a small notch (painted arrows). From here, the trail leads to the summit.

Continue over to the north summit, where you will find one of the largest cairns you've ever seen.

For the descent, reverse the route, possibly staying more on the climbers' trail, for speed.

From the small notch, looking up to the summit. The trail skirts the cliffs on the left side.

40. Mount Neva—North Ridge

The north ridge of Mount Neva, seen from South Arapaho Peak.

ROUND-TRIP DISTANCE	9 miles
ROUND-TRIP TIME	6 to 7 hours
STARTING ELEVATION	10,172 feet
HIGHEST ELEVATION	12,814 feet
ELEVATION GAIN	3,400 feet
SEASON	Late June to October
JURISDICTION	Roosevelt National Forest, Boulder Ranger District, Indian Peaks Wilderness
MAPS	Monarch Lake 7.5 minute; East Portal 7.5 minute

OVERVIEW: A trail hike to the ridge. Good scrambling on relatively solid rock. Mostly Class 2 and 3 with two short Class 4 sections.

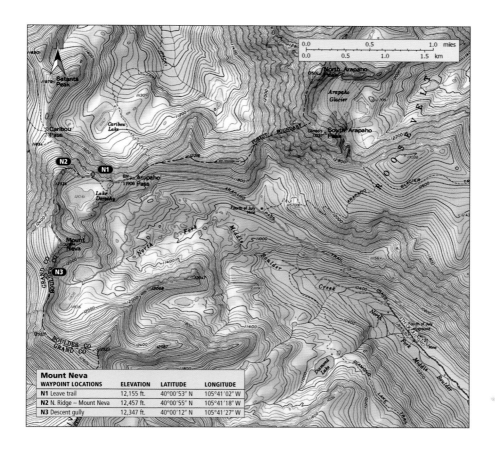

Mount Neva			
WAYPOINT LOCATIONS	**ELEVATION**	**LATITUDE**	**LONGITUDE**
N1 Leave trail	12,155 ft.	40°00'53" N	105°41'02" W
N2 N. Ridge – Mount Neva	12,457 ft.	40°00'55" N	105°41'18" W
N3 Descent gully	12,347 ft.	40°00'12" N	105°41'27" W

GETTING THERE: From Nederland (west of Boulder on Colorado 119), drive west on Colorado 119 to the Eldora junction at the edge of town. Turn right here and head west, staying straight after 1.4 miles where the road to the Eldora Ski Area takes off to the left. At 4 miles, the road turns to dirt (shortly after passing through the town of Eldora). Continue to the Buckingham Campground (shown on the map as the Fourth of July Campground) at 8.8 miles. Trailhead parking is just uphill from the campground.

COMMENT: This fine route is a delight. Good rock, fun scrambling, and great views make this a classic.

APPROACH: From the trailhead (TH) at Buckingham Campground, head up the Arapaho Pass Trail for 3 miles to Arapaho Pass. Take the left-hand fork on the Caribou Pass Trail until leaving the trail at N1 (12,155 feet),

Scrambling on an early section of the ridge.

and head west up the gentle ridge to intersect the north ridge of Mount Neva at N2.

ROUTE DESCRIPTION: The ridge south to the summit of Mount Neva is 0.7 mile, usually on Class 2 and 3 terrain. While there is a cairned trail some distance below the ridge, the ridge crest provides a very enjoyable scramble, so head up the ridge.

Solid rock makes for excellent climbing, and you can make rapid progress along the ridge. At the first significant notch, drop to the left (east) of the ridge and climb down into the notch.

At the first crux, scramble up to the base of an obvious dihedral, just right of a rock rib. The next 40 feet provide very nice Class 4 climbing, or bypass this section and climb grassy steps to the left of the rib.

At the top of this section, continue along the narrow ridge and almost immediately downclimb into a narrow notch. Getting out of the notch constitutes the next crux, although it is not as difficult as the section you have just climbed.

Traverse left on ledges for a few feet until you can climb up a slot for perhaps 20 feet (Class 4).

Once you are past this section, the difficulties ease significantly for the remainder of the climb to the summit.

To descend from the summit, continue toward Jasper (south along the connecting ridge) until you reach a reasonable descent gully (N3). Descend to a bench between two unnamed lakes. The goal is to traverse back to the ascent trail, avoiding cliff bands, willows, and marshes. The map shows one route that works. Don't drop all the way into the drainage, however, or you'll definitely find the willows and marshes.

An alternative descent route reverses the north ridge, possibly using the cairned trail to bypass some of the difficulties you just overcame.

Gary checking out the first crux.

41. Lone Eagle Peak

An impressive view of Lone Eagle from camp at Crater Lake.

ROUND-TRIP DISTANCE	13.8 miles backpacking; 3 miles scrambling
ROUND-TRIP TIME	5 hours from camp at Crater Lake
STARTING ELEVATION	8,376 feet
HIGHEST ELEVATION	12,000 feet
ELEVATION GAIN	2,900 feet backpacking; 3,000 feet scrambling
SEASON	Late June to September
JURISDICTION	Roosevelt National Forest, Sulpher Ranger District, Indian Peaks Wilderness
MAP	Monarch Lake 7.5 minute

OVERVIEW: A long backpack to a camp at Crater Lake, with an exposed scramble (Class 4) to an amazing summit on good rock.

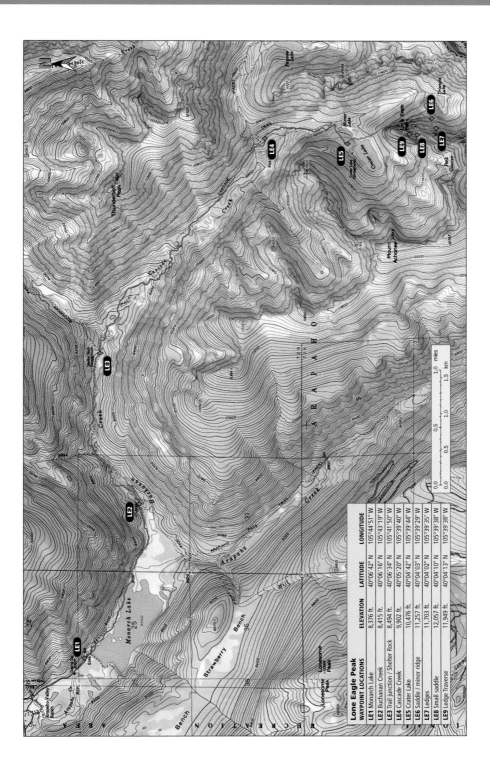

Lone Eagle Peak		
WAYPOINT LOCATIONS	ELEVATION	LATITUDE	LONGITUDE
LE1 Monarch Lake	8,376 ft.	40°06'42" N	105°44'51" W
LE2 Buchanan Creek	8,415 ft.	40°06'16" N	105°43'19" W
LE3 Trail junction / Shelter Rock	8,494 ft.	40°06'34" N	105°41'50" W
LE4 Cascade Creek	9,902 ft.	40°05'20" N	105°39'40" W
LE5 Crater Lake	10,476 ft.	40°04'42" N	105°39'44" W
LE6 Saddle / minor ridge	11,257 ft.	40°04'03" N	105°39'29" W
LE7 Ledges	11,703 ft.	40°04'02" N	105°39'35" W
LE8 Small saddle	12,057 ft.	40°04'10" N	105°39'38" W
LE9 Ledge Traverse	11,949 ft.	40°04'13" N	105°39'38" W

Starting the long backpack to Crater Lake.

GETTING THERE: From the junction of U.S. 40 and U.S. 34, on the northern edge of Granby, head northeast on U.S. 34 for 5.4 miles. Turn east (right) onto the road signed to Arapaho Bay and follow it for 10.4 miles along the south shore of Lake Granby to the trailhead parking area (LE1).

COMMENT: This great peak is one of the few peaks you'll climb where the summit is undeniably not the high point of the ridge. Nevertheless, it makes a fine scramble, even by its easiest route.

APPROACH: From the parking area at Monarch Lake (LE1), take the trail for 6.9 miles to Crater Lake (LE5). The views are spectacular!

From the saddle above Triangle Lake, look for a right-angling gully immediately under the black-streaked cliffs.

ROUTE DESCRIPTION: From the camping areas near the northeast end of Crater Lake, cross the outlet on a logjam and aim for the prow of Lone Eagle Peak, making use of a climbers' trail if possible. As you approach the cliffs of the peak, angle left (east), staying close to the cliffs. A cairned trail continues along the east edge of the peak until reaching the right-most (upper) saddle (LE6) on a minor ridge at 11,257 feet, 0.9 mile from Crater Lake. This saddle overlooks Triangle Lake.

Note that a cairned trail continues southwest for some distance beyond this point. This is not the best way to go. The photo above shows the view from the saddle. Look for a right-angling gully immediately under the distinctive black-streaked cliffs seen to the left of center in the photo. This Class 2 gully leads northwest to a series of ledges (LE7) and a clearly visible cairned route that zigzags up toward the towers on the ridge before heading north to hit the ridge at a small saddle (LE8), where the downward path to the summit is revealed.

Follow the climbers' trail as it drops 15 feet onto the west side of the ridge, then contours back for perhaps 50 feet to reach a small notch in the

Heading up from the saddle above Triangle Lake.

Lone Eagle's summit is at the right end of the ridge—approximate route shown in red.

ridge blocked by a chockstone. Easily climb over the chockstone.

Once you are over the chockstone, traverse on ledges to a point (LE9) where you must either downclimb a Class 4 pitch or rappel (50-meter rope is adequate). If you use a rope, consider leaving it in place for the return journey.

From the broad ledges, again follow a trail to a point below the summit pinnacle. Choose a route to the summit.

To descend, reverse the route.

Looking back along the summit ridge.

42. Navajo Peak

Navajo Peak.

ROUND-TRIP DISTANCE	9.6 miles
ROUND-TRIP TIME	7 hours
STARTING ELEVATION	10,541 feet
HIGHEST ELEVATION	13,409 feet
ELEVATION GAIN	3,200 feet
SEASON	Late June to October
JURISDICTION	Roosevelt National Forest, Boulder Ranger District; Indian Peaks Wilderness
MAPS	Monarch Lake 7.5 minute; Ward 7.5 minute

OVERVIEW: A trail hike, followed by off-trail, Class 2 scrambling to the summit block. A few Class 3 moves on ledges get you to the summit.

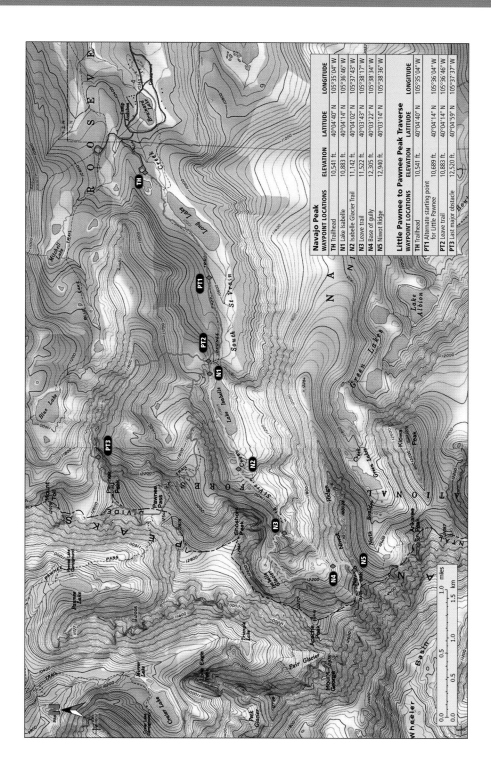

Navajo Peak

WAYPOINT LOCATIONS	ELEVATION	LATITUDE	LONGITUDE
TH Trailhead	10,541 ft.	40°04'40" N	105°35'04" W
N1 Lake Isabelle	10,883 ft.	40°04'14" N	105°36'46" W
N2 Isabelle Glacier Trail	11,142 ft.	40°04'02" N	105°37'43" W
N3 Leave trail	11,522 ft.	40°03'43" N	105°38'17" W
N4 Base of gully	12,305 ft.	40°03'22" N	105°38'34" W
N5 Niwot Ridge	12,940 ft.	40°03'14" N	105°38'36" W

Little Pawnee to Pawnee Peak Traverse

WAYPOINT LOCATIONS	ELEVATION	LATITUDE	LONGITUDE
TH Trailhead	10,541 ft.	40°04'40" N	105°35'04" W
PT1 Alternate starting point for Little Pawnee	10,689 ft.	40°04'14" N	105°36'04" W
PT2 Leave trail	10,883 ft.	40°04'14" N	105°36'46" W
PT3 Last major obstacle	12,520 ft.	40°04'59" N	105°37'37" W

View of direct route from N3. Aim for the low point on the foreground ridge, to access Airplane Gully.

GETTING THERE: Go 12.1 miles north of Nederland (0.4 mile north of the turnoff to Ward) on Colorado 72, and turn left (west) on the road into the Indian Peaks Wilderness. Follow the signs to the Long Lake Trailhead.

COMMENT: One of the most impressive peaks in the Indian Peaks Wilderness, Navajo offers several fine snow and rock routes. The route described here is a fun, interesting, moderate route. The difficulty never exceeds Class 3, even on the imposing summit block.

APPROACH: From the Long Lake Trailhead, take the Isabelle Glacier Trail past Isabelle Lake and along South St. Vrain Creek to a small, unnamed lake at 11,430 feet.

Leave the trail (N3) at the unnamed lake, 3.5 miles from the trailhead, where it climbs steeply north into the basin below the Isabelle Glacier.

Airplane Gully is the weakness seen near the center of photo.

Contour around the north then west side of the lake, and ascend large boulders into the bowl directly below Navajo. A climbers' trail with occasional cairns may be found that can help you get through some minor rock bands below the basin.

Navajo's imposing summit. The route ascends the east face, at left of photo.

The map also shows an alternate approach to the upper basin, allowing you to stay on the trail longer. This adds quite a bit of distance to the approach.

ROUTE DESCRIPTION: Once you are in the upper basin at about 12,200 feet, look for a north-facing gully that provides access to Niwot Ridge. This gully, known as Airplane Gully, has debris strewn about from a crash that occurred more than 50 years ago. Large sections of the fuselage are still intact.

Head for the base of this gully (N4) and scramble up the reasonably stable slope. Near the top of the gully it divides, with the best route veering right, just past the major part of the aircraft debris. This brings you out on top of Niwot Ridge (N5).

From here, head west along the ridge to the base of Navajo's summit block.

A climbers' trail ascends the east face. Follow this upward until the summit cliffs halt your progress. Angle up and to the left on ledges and turn the corner. From here, it is a simple scramble to the summit.

Reverse the route to descend.

43. Little Pawnee to Pawnee Peak Traverse

The ridge from Little Pawnee to Pawnee Peak, seen from just below the summit of Pawnee Peak.

ROUND-TRIP DISTANCE	8.7 miles
ROUND-TRIP TIME	7 to 8 hours
STARTING ELEVATION	10,541 feet
HIGHEST ELEVATION	12,943 feet
ELEVATION GAIN	2,700 feet
SEASON	Late June to October
JURISDICTION	Roosevelt National Forest, Boulder Ranger District; Indian Peaks Wilderness
MAPS	Monarch Lake 7.5 minute; Ward 7.5 minute

OVERVIEW: A trail approach followed by off-trail scrambling to the east ridge of Little Pawnee Peak. A complex ridge traverse to Pawnee Peak with plenty of Class 3 and 4 scrambling.

SEE MAP PAGE 239

GETTING THERE: Go 12.1 miles north of Nederland (0.4 mile north of the turnoff to Ward) on Colorado 72, then turn left (west) on the road into the Indian Peaks Wilderness. Follow the signs to the Long Lake Trailhead.

COMMENT: This traverse is really the east ridge of Pawnee Peak and is the most interesting way to climb Pawnee Peak. Route finding on this ridge is a significant challenge, so although the climb isn't long, it's definitely worthwhile.

APPROACH: Getting onto the east ridge of Little Pawnee Peak is a bushwhack, no matter how you do it. The easiest climbing is by an approach from the west end of Long Lake. However, this involves wandering through

Carefully pick your way down the ridge from the summit of Little Pawnee.

Looking back at the downclimb off Little Pawnee's summit.

the trees for quite some distance. Another approach is to go to Lake Isabelle and catch a ridge descending from Little Pawnee's east ridge directly toward the lake. A variation to this approach is to head up just before reaching the lake (PT2). Either of these latter two approaches is reasonable and involves Class 2 and 3 scrambling through minor cliff bands. The lower parts of these routes are on loose talus, so be careful.

From the Long Lake Trailhead, walk up the Pawnee Pass Trail to the appropriate departure point and gain the east ridge of Little Pawnee.

ROUTE DESCRIPTION: The scramble to the summit of Little Pawnee is straightforward, but then the fun begins.

The downclimb from the summit of Little Pawnee goes at Class 3 or 4 and requires careful route finding. This is the crux of the route. The best line of descent stays on or close to the nose of the ridge.

Climb over or around the next obstacle. If you elect to bypass it, traverse on the right (north) side of the ridge. This brings you to a couple of steep towers that are best passed on the right.

Regain the ridge (PT3) and attack the last obstacle, climbing its right shoulder. The difficulties are essentially over. Drop down to avoid a notch in the ridge, then follow the ridgeline to the summit of Pawnee Peak.

For the descent, drop down to the Pawnee Pass Trail (south) and take it back to the trailhead.

Scenic scrambling along the ridge.   PHOTO BY CHARLIE WINGER

Rocky Mountain National Park

The Spearhead, in Rocky Mountain National Park.

Rocky Mountain National Park contains the highest concentration of quality technical, alpine rock climbs in the state. Scattered among these impressive technical faces there are also some fine scrambles. This guide offers a selection for your enjoyment.

There are several distinct areas comprising the park. All of the climbs described here are accessed from the east side. Routes on Longs Peak are approached from the Longs Peak Ranger Station, while the routes further north are accessed from Estes Park.

Estes Park caters to hordes of tourists during the summer months, so all amenities are provided. There are plenty of private campgrounds in the area: several on the Fall River Road, near the entrance to the park. Camping is also available in the park itself.

Miles of granite.

THE ROCK

Nothing but granite! A huge expanse of an exposed granite batholith, heavily glaciated, forms steep, solid, rock faces. While this isn't true of the rock at the northern end of the park, the scrambles described here avoid that area, for good reason.

44. Mount Meeker and Longs Peak Via The Loft and Clark's Arrow

The Meeker/Longs Cirque.

ROUND-TRIP DISTANCE	13.3 miles
ROUND-TRIP TIME	12 hours
STARTING ELEVATION	9,398 feet
HIGHEST ELEVATION	14,255 feet
ELEVATION GAIN	6,300 feet
SEASON	June to September
JURISDICTION	Rocky Mountain National Park
MAPS	Longs Peak 7.5 minute; Allenspark 7.5 minute

OVERVIEW: A long approach (no pun intended), Class 3 scrambling to the Loft, mainly Class 2 scrambling to the summit of Meeker, and mostly Class 3 with a little Class 4 scrambling on the Clark's Arrow Route to the summit of Longs. Depending on the descent route chosen, a rappel might be required.

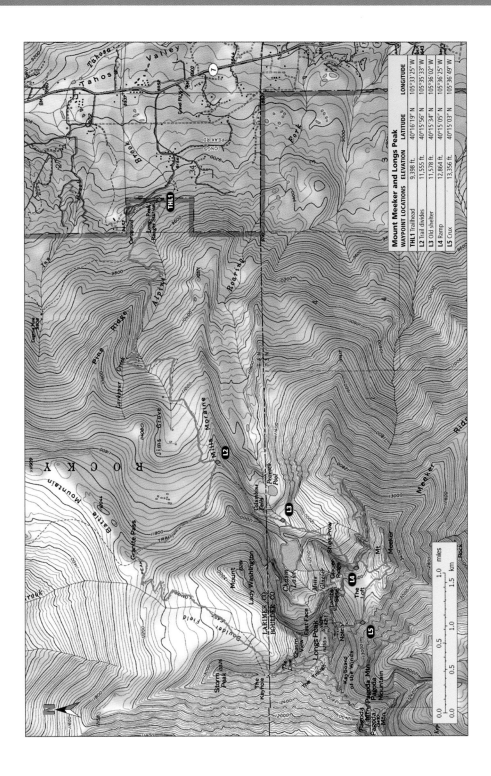

Mount Meeker and Longs Peak

WAYPOINT LOCATIONS	ELEVATION	LATITUDE	LONGITUDE
THL1 Trailhead	9,398 ft.	40°16'19" N	105°33'25" W
L2 Trail divides	11,555 ft.	40°15'56" N	105°35'33" W
L3 Old shelter	11,578 ft.	40°15'34" N	105°36'02" W
L4 Ramp	12,864 ft.	40°15'05" N	105°36'25" W
L5 Crux	13,356 ft.	40°15'03" N	105°36'49" W

Dwight scrambling up towards the Loft.

On the ramp used to bypass the headwall at the top of the Loft.

Downclimbing the narrow gully (crux) before reaching Clark's Arrow.

GETTING THERE: Go 8.7 miles south of Estes Park on Colorado 7 or 20.6 miles north of Ward on Colorado 7, then turn west for a mile toward the Longs Peak Ranger Station. Park here. Do not park overnight without a backcountry permit or you will be ticketed.

COMMENT: This route is an excellent way to combine the normal route up Meeker with a great, less-traveled route on Longs Peak. Clark's Arrow Route is not much harder than the Keyhole (standard) Route but is a much more aesthetic mountain experience than the often-crowded Keyhole Route. Unlike the Keyhole Route, this

Clark's Arrow can be seen above the upper climber's head on this less-than-perfect day. The climbers are travelling in the opposite direction from the route described here.

scramble provides more of a route-finding challenge.

There are two commonly used descent routes: the north face (Cables Route) or the Keyhole Route. The Cables Route requires at least one rappel. Here I describe the less technical Keyhole descent.

APPROACH: From the trailhead, take the Longs Peak Trail for 3.1 miles to the point where it divides on Mills Moraine (L2). Continue on the trail along the left (southwest) branch to just below Chasm Lake, reaching the rebuilt shelter where the trail becomes a climbers' trail (L3).

ROUTE DESCRIPTION: Head up toward the Loft (the obvious low point between Longs and Meeker) on a rough climbers' trail. This is a snow climb for much of the summer and Class 3 scrambling on slabs later in the season.

At waypoint L4, just below the steep headwall, a ramp allows escape from the gully and avoids the steeper climbing on the right side of the headwall. Follow the ramp as it heads left, then climb back to the right to gain the Loft. The views from the ramp are amazing.

Once you are at the Loft, it is a simple scramble left on a climbers' trail and narrow ridge to the summit of Mount Meeker.

Looking back at Clark's Arrow, shown in inset.

Return to the Loft and follow a cairned trail as it descends slightly to the west corner of the Loft. From here, continue on the cairned trail on a descending traverse across the head of a broad gully. Look for a small saddle on the northwest side of this gully, marked by a cairn.

Drop down from this saddle into a narrow, steep gully (L5), the crux of the route.

Downclimb approximately 100 feet until you can exit right onto ledges. Continue north around the corner and look behind and slightly above you. You should see Clark's Arrow painted on the rock.

Continue north on a climbers' trail, staying to the right side of the couloir (Keplinger's Couloir) and aiming for the Notch at its head.

Just below the Notch, contour onto the obvious ramp and make a rising traverse to join the Homestretch.

Once you are on the Homestretch, follow the red and yellow bull's-eyes to the summit plateau.

To descend the Keyhole Route, retrace your steps down the Homestretch, but this time continue on the Keyhole Route as it heads northwest across the Narrows and down the top of the Trough, then parallels Longs' northwest ridge to the Keyhole. The route is well marked with the famous bull's-eyes.

From the Keyhole, descend onto the Boulder Field and traverse northeast to rejoin the East Longs Peak Trail.

One comment about the Keyhole Route: In winter conditions it is considered to be a technical route, mainly due to ice flows that form along the route. This can happen as early as mid-September.

Looking up at Longs from Clark's Arrow—the Homestretch can be seen near top of photo. The Notch is to the right, out of view. The ice drips visible are directly below the ramp that connects with the Homestretch.

Traversing the Narrows section while descending the Keyhole route.

45. Little Matterhorn

Little Matterhorn. The route reaches the ridge near the left side of the photo.

ROUND-TRIP DISTANCE	8.4 miles
ROUND-TRIP TIME	6 to 7 hours
STARTING ELEVATION	9,453 feet
HIGHEST ELEVATION	11,621 feet
ELEVATION GAIN	2,800 feet
SEASON	June through October
JURISDICTION	Rocky Mountain National Park
MAP	McHenrys Peak 7.5 minute

OVERVIEW: Approach on a good trail. Scramble up talus slopes to the ridge, with a short, complex scramble to a unique summit with an optional, challenging downclimb to the end of the ridge.

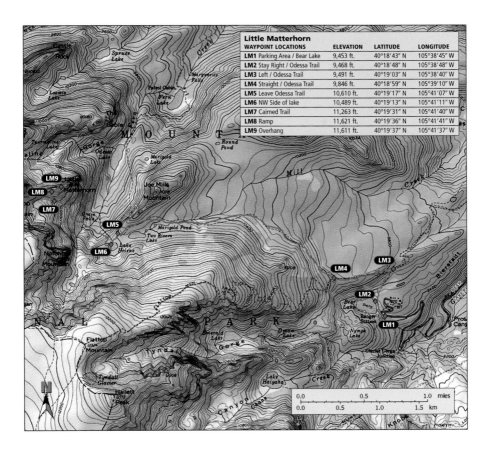

Little Matterhorn			
WAYPOINT LOCATIONS	ELEVATION	LATITUDE	LONGITUDE
LM1 Parking Area / Bear Lake	9,453 ft.	40°18'43" N	105°38'45" W
LM2 Stay Right / Odessa Trail	9,468 ft.	40°18'48" N	105°38'48" W
LM3 Left / Odessa Trail	9,491 ft.	40°19'03" N	105°38'40" W
LM4 Straight / Odessa Trail	9,846 ft.	40°18'59" N	105°39'10" W
LM5 Leave Odessa Trail	10,610 ft.	40°19'17" N	105°41'07" W
LM6 NW Side of lake	10,489 ft.	40°19'13" N	105°41'11" W
LM7 Cairned Trail	11,263 ft.	40°19'31" N	105°41'40" W
LM8 Ramp	11,621 ft.	40°19'36" N	105°41'41" W
LM9 Overhang	11,611 ft.	40°19'37" N	105°41'37" W

GETTING THERE: From the major intersection of U.S. Highways 34 and 36 in the town of Estes Park, head west through town on U.S. 36. Turn south in 0.4 mile and continue on U.S. 36 as it turns west to Rocky Mountain National Park. Turn left (south) on Bear Lake Road after 4.4 miles and drive to its terminus at the large parking area, a total of 14 miles.

Consider using the shuttle bus rather than driving to Bear Lake. For more information go to: http://www.nps.gov/romo/visit/shuttle.html.

COMMENT: This relatively short scramble is lots of fun. Little Matterhorn is actually the east ridge of Knobtop Mountain, and, like Lone Eagle, the objective is the end of the ridge, rather than the high point. In fact, the crux of the route is reaching a large cairn on a point just beyond the "end" of the ridge. I recommend not eating your lunch until after negotiating this squeeze chimney.

Approaching the ridge; the ramp providing access to the ridge is at far right of photo.

Working the way along the ridge.

APPROACH: From the Bear Lake parking area, take the Odessa Lake Trail, staying right at LM2, left at LM3, and straight ahead (right) at LM4.

ROUTE DESCRIPTION: At LM5, leave the Odessa Lake Trail at the sharp right-hand bend in the trail. Head left to Lake Helene and follow the trail as it skirts the right side of the lake. At LM6, on the northwest side of the lake, look for a trail taking off to your right. This is a reasonably good trail heading to Grace Falls.

Climbing up the squeeze chimney.

After switchbacking down the hill, the trail peters out. Head for the obvious talus slope below Little Matterhorn, staying left of the cliff band at the base.

Work your way up and right into the gully between Little Matterhorn and Knobtop. Head up the gully until above the rock slabs. Various cairned trails exist. LM7 marks the start of one variation.

Find a way onto the ridge. A ramp (LM8) provides perhaps the easiest way up. After that, make your way along the ridge, dropping down in one spot to avoid an overhang (LM9).

Depending on your line along the ridge, the climbing will be either Class 3 or 4. It is best to avoid the potential for Class 5. The squeeze chimney at the end of the ridge is difficult—at least Class 4—so take care.

Descend the same way you ascended.

46. McHenrys Peak—Southeast Ridge

McHenrys Peak. The Stoneman, for which the pass at the center of photo is named, can be seen to the left of the pass.

ROUND-TRIP DISTANCE	12.5 miles
ROUND-TRIP TIME	9 to 10 hours
STARTING ELEVATION	9,213 feet
HIGHEST ELEVATION	13,327 feet
ELEVATION GAIN	4,200 feet
SEASON	June to September
JURISDICTION	Rocky Mountain National Park
MAP	McHenrys Peak 7.5 minute

OVERVIEW: A long trail approach with challenging scrambling on the upper part of the route.

GETTING THERE: From the major intersection of U.S. Highways 34 and 36 in the town of Estes Park, head west through town on U.S. 36. Turn south in 0.4 mile and continue on U.S. 36 as it turns west to Rocky Mountain National Park. Turn left (south) on Bear Lake Road after 4.4 miles and drive to the Glacier Gorge Parking Area and Trailhead, a total of 12.7 miles

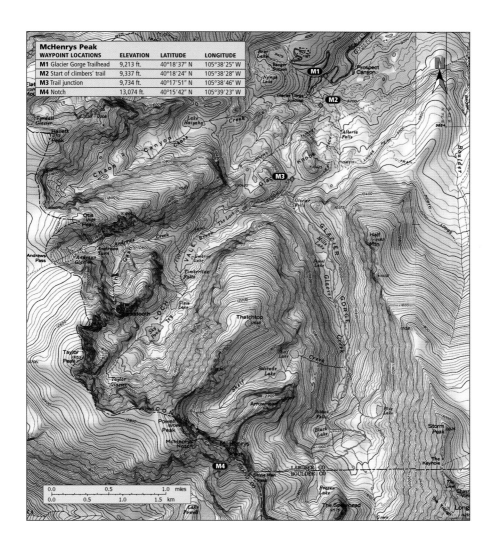

McHenrys Peak WAYPOINT LOCATIONS	ELEVATION	LATITUDE	LONGITUDE
M1 Glacier Gorge Trailhead	9,213 ft.	40°18′37″ N	105°38′25″ W
M2 Start of climbers' trail	9,337 ft.	40°18′24″ N	105°38′28″ W
M3 Trail junction	9,734 ft.	40°17′51″ N	105°38′46″ W
M4 Notch	13,074 ft.	40°15′42″ N	105°39′23″ W

Consider using the shuttle bus rather than driving to Glacier Gorge. For more information go to: http://www.nps.gov/romo/visit/shuttle.html.

COMMENT: McHenrys has the reputation of being the most difficult of the high peaks in Rocky Mountain National Park (by the standard route). Whether or not this is the case, the standard route described here is a fine mountaineering challenge. When this route is climbed early in the season, snow will certainly be encountered, and by September, new snow and ice will present even more of a challenge. The summit provides some route-finding difficulties, so I've included more detail in this description.

The gully leading to Stoneman Pass.

PHOTO BY CHARLIE WINGER

View after reaching Stoneman Pass. The red arrow marks the notch used to gain the upper mountain.

Closeup of notch.

APPROACH: From the Glacier Gorge Trailhead (M1), head up toward Black Lake and Mills Lake. Most climbers take the unmarked climbers' access shortcut, which saves about 0.6 mile each way. When you are 0.45 mile from the trailhead, look for the large split rock on a slab (M2) for the start of the climbers' trail. This trail rejoins the main trail just before the trail junction (M3), where the right fork heads to Loch Vale. We head left here. Continue past Mills Lake to Black Lake.

ROUTE DESCRIPTION: At Black Lake you have a choice. Either head directly up the slabs west of the lake, or continue on a trail as it heads east up the drainage above the lake. (A word of caution—the slabs west of the lake can be quite difficult to negotiate, especially when wet or icy—which is often the case.) Assuming that you opt for the trail east from the lake, follow

The ledge immediately past the notch. Climb the short face to the right to access the gully above.

cairns as they circle back to the west above cliffs encircling Black Lake. If you don't find this cairned trail, the low vegetation will be a challenge to negotiate (ask me how I know!). The cairns lead you across the drainage below Frozen Lake and across a vast expanse of granite slabs to the beginning of the gully leading to Stoneman Pass. Approach the gully from the left, bypassing a small cliff band below the gully.

Scramble up loose scree (or snow, depending on the season) to the pass. There are two routes from here. One traverses northwest on a well-marked trail and then climbs steeply. The other (also cairned) follows the ridgeline

Looking back across the top of the gully, from near the summit. The cairn on top of the ridge indicates a more serious route which avoids the notch. Chiefs Head can be seen in the background.

more closely. This latter provides more scrambling. The two routes join a little higher, below a notch in a prominent ridge (M4).

Cross the notch and immediately find yourself on a flat ledge. The route climbs straight up the rock face to your right on a series of small ledges.

This provides access to a broad gully. Follow cairns (several lines) up the gully to a point a little below the ridgeline, then traverse left and up to meet the south ridge before heading to the summit.

Descend the ascent route.

Clear Creek Section

High winds are common in the Clear Creek Range.

This compact section of the Front Range covers the section south of the Indian Peaks Wilderness and north of Guanella Pass.

The proximity of this range to Denver makes the area very popular, but the routes described here, while well known to mountaineers, are less traveled.

The Sawtooth Ridge extending from Mount Evans to Mount Bierstadt was my first ridge-scrambling traverse. It makes a good introduction to ridge running.

My ascents of the Kelso ridge on Torreys Peak number in the teens; the outing makes a good training climb in any season of the year.

The Citadel, while not a high peak, owes its fame to its prominent position north of I-70 as well as its striking features.

Bancroft, in the James Peak group, is one of several worthy climbs in the area, and it is accessible year-round.

Fractured rock on the Citadel.

THE ROCK

More of the Precambrian igneous and metamorphic schist and gneiss found in much of the Front Range. The rock quality varies from the solid granite of the Mount Evans area to the fractured rock found on the Citadel.

47. Mount Bierstadt to Mount Evans— Sawtooth Ridge

The Sawtooth Ridge connects Mount Bierstadt to Mount Evans.

ROUND-TRIP DISTANCE	9.9 miles
ROUND-TRIP TIME	10 hours
STARTING ELEVATION	11,674 feet
HIGHEST ELEVATION	14,260 feet
ELEVATION GAIN	4,650 feet
SEASON	June to October
JURISDICTION	Arapaho National Forest, Clear Creek Ranger District, Mount Evans Wilderness
MAP	Mount Evans 7.5 minute

OVERVIEW: An easy trail up Mount Bierstadt followed by a fun scramble over the Sawtooth to the long west ridge of Mount Evans. Easy scrambling takes you to the summit of Mount Evans. Return by retracing your steps down the west ridge of Mount Evans, then over Mount Spalding via easy off-trail walking.

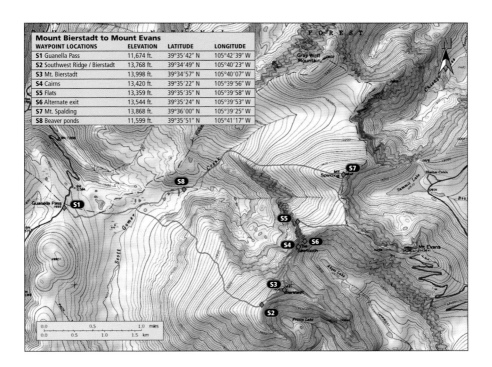

Mount Bierstadt to Mount Evans			
WAYPOINT LOCATIONS	ELEVATION	LATITUDE	LONGITUDE
S1 Guanella Pass	11,674 ft.	39°35'42" N	105°42'39" W
S2 Southwest Ridge / Bierstadt	13,768 ft.	39°34'49" N	105°40'23" W
S3 Mt. Bierstadt	13,998 ft.	39°34'57" N	105°40'07" W
S4 Cairns	13,420 ft.	39°35'22" N	105°39'56" W
S5 Flats	13,359 ft.	39°35'35" N	105°39'58" W
S6 Alternate exit	13,544 ft.	39°35'24" N	105°39'53" W
S7 Mt. Spalding	13,868 ft.	39°36'00" N	105°39'25" W
S8 Beaver ponds	11,599 ft.	39°35'51" N	105°41'17" W

GETTING THERE: The trailhead is at the top of Guanella Pass and can be reached by heading 10 miles south from Georgetown off Interstate 70 at exit 228 or north from Grant off U.S. 285 for 13 miles.

COMMENT: The Sawtooth Ridge is one of the classic Fourteener traverses and is by far the easiest, hence a good introduction to scrambling. A good trail installed across the dreaded willows by the Colorado Fourteeners Initiative has made the start of this trip much more pleasant. Prior to that, it was quite common to don gaiters in the hope that these would keep the mud at bay.

APPROACH: From the south end of the parking area at the top of the pass (S1), follow the well-worn trail as it drops about 100 feet into the willows. Crossing the shallow valley of Scott Gomer Creek and emerging on the far side of the willows, the trail climbs southeast up the gentle, tundra-clad, west slopes of Mount Bierstadt via switchbacks, reaching the southwest ridge of Bierstadt at 13,768 feet (S2). From here, walk northeast up the easy ridge to the summit (S3).

View of the Sawtooth from the summit of Mount Bierstadt.

ROUTE DESCRIPTION: From the summit of Mount Bierstadt, the Sawtooth ridge looks quite impressive (don't they all?). This is a good place to take a break and decide which way you will go. Also, admire Abyss Lake, 1,400 feet below you to the northeast.

After dropping down off Mount Bierstadt's northeast ridge over large, stable blocks, you will see a trail on the southeast side of the ridge, below the rocky ridge proper. This will take you most of the way across but hardly counts as "doing the ridge." By staying as close to the ridge crest as possible most of the time, the difficulty stays at Class 3. Climb over or bypass several pinnacles on the southeast side on very reasonable ledge systems until you are in the Sawtooth proper (the last third of the crossing).

The key to the traverse is finding the large, scree- and boulder-strewn ramp that contours beneath the bold cliffs guarding the end of the Sawtooth. At a set of cairns between the last two major pinnacles (S4), cross from the south to the north side of the ridge. From this saddle, a faint trail contours to the north for 100 feet, past some car-sized boulders and then over loose scree, before turning northwest under the end of the

Sawtooth. This section can hold snow well into the summer. A wide ramp system, amply marked with cairns, angles upward as you continue northwest for 200 feet, finally depositing you on the flats (S5).

Scrambling on the ramp exiting the Sawtooth. PHOTO BY TERRY ROOT

If you missed the turnoff from the ridge, or simply want a more challenging scramble, an alternate route down to the ramp presents itself after passing the last pinnacle on the Sawtooth. Once again, cairns mark the spot (S6) where a much narrower ledge winds left and down from the ridge, joining the ramp system at its low point, just prior to the climb up to the flats. If you are planning on returning by way of the Sawtooth, make note of the spot where the ramp exits onto the flats, as this key feature is harder to spot going from Mount Evans to Mount Bierstadt.

The summit of Mount Evans is one mile away, east across the flats, then along its west ridge. It is worth making this detour to surprise the tourists atop one of Colorado's most frequented peaks (possibly due to the presence of the road?). Actually, the ridge offers some fun, Class 2 scrambling on solid slabs and hopping over boulders.

From Mount Evans, return along the west ridge to the point where you must decide whether to retrace your steps across the Sawtooth or circle around to the north past Mount Spalding. Assuming that you choose the scenic route, you may as well bag Spalding while you're at it, so head north on gentle terrain to the summit. Unfortunately, Mount Spalding (S7) doesn't count as a separate peak by the definition usually applied, since the

Looking back along the Sawtooth Ridge after exiting the ramp.   PHOTO BY TERRY ROOT

saddle between it and Evans only drops 268 feet, but it is a named peak over 13,800 feet.

Descend grassy slopes along Spalding's west ridge, staying north of the cliffs guarding the headwaters of Scott Gomer Creek. Since you don't have the benefit of the nice trail through the willows that you used on the approach, you must now choose your bushwhack route. In general, bear west, staying on a small ridge that deposits you by a series of small beaver ponds (S8). From here, head southwest directly back toward the parking area.

48. Torreys Peak— Northeast Ridge (Kelso Ridge)

The Kelso Ridge of Torreys Peak forms the left skyline.

ROUND-TRIP DISTANCE	6.5 miles from summer trailhead
ROUND-TRIP TIME	6 hours
STARTING ELEVATION	11,246 feet
HIGHEST ELEVATION	14,267 feet
ELEVATION GAIN	3,100 feet
SEASON	Year-round, but usually June through October
JURISDICTION	Arapaho National Forest, Clear Creek Ranger District
MAP	Grays Peak 7.5 minute

OVERVIEW: An easy trail walk to approach the saddle. Moderate scrambling along the ridge with short sections of exposed scrambling in one or two spots. Descent from the summit is on good trails with glissading options.

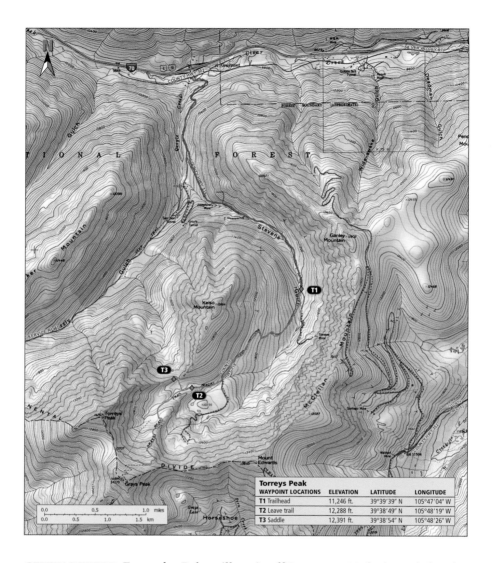

Torreys Peak			
WAYPOINT LOCATIONS	**ELEVATION**	**LATITUDE**	**LONGITUDE**
T1 Trailhead	11,246 ft.	39°39'39" N	105°47'04" W
T2 Leave trail	12,288 ft.	39°38'49" N	105°48'19" W
T3 Saddle	12,391 ft.	39°38'54" N	105°48'26" W

GETTING THERE: From the Bakerville exit off Interstate 70 (exit 221), head south up the Stevens Gulch Road for 3 miles on the rocky dirt road to the fenced parking area at 11,246 feet (T1).

COMMENT: This ridge can be climbed at any time of the year and is often used as training by those preparing for an expedition. Since the road up Stevens Gulch is closed by snow typically from November into May, winter ascents are significantly longer and more committing. While this route can be done in one day from Interstate-70, many parties prefer to pack in some distance. Camping just below the saddle at the 12,300-foot level can provide the aspiring alpinist with quite extreme conditions. More than one group has been happy to head down at first light after a miserable night spent here, abandoning any thoughts of doing the climb!

Approaching the Torreys-Kelso saddle, seen at right in this photo.

Remember that in winter conditions this route is a much more serious undertaking than in summer season conditions. Be prepared to belay short sections, and take crampons as well as your ice ax. Try it in the summer before planning your winter outing.

APPROACH: From the trailhead (T1), head south across the metal bridge on the well-worn Grays Peak Trail. Follow this trail for 2 miles as it passes Kelso Mountain until you are just south of the saddle connecting Torreys Peak with Kelso Mountain at about 12,300 feet (T2). Note that in winter or early spring conditions, slides regularly come off Kelso and cross the trail.

ROUTE DESCRIPTION:
Leave the trail at T2 and head toward the saddle (T3) on a faint trail. Note the old mine at this saddle. This route has become increasingly popular in recent years, creating a fairly well-defined trail along much of the ridge.

The route always stays within 20 feet or

View of the ridge from the Torreys-Kelso saddle.

The first difficulty after starting up the ridge from the saddle.

so of the ridge crest, switching sides frequently or staying on top. There are sections of easy walking interspersed with Class 3 scrambling over short obstacles; however, these obstacles generally offer plenty of solid handholds and footholds. Either climb directly over or bypass these obstacles.

On one late March ascent, the lower part of the ridge went quite slowly due to a considerable amount of new snow on the route, making route finding challenging. The upper part of the route went much more smoothly when I encountered mountain goat tracks. The critter showed impeccable route-finding ability.

Continue up to the 14,000-foot level, where one last tower deposits you at the top of the Dead Dog Couloir. A steep, rocky outcrop of light gray rock provides the most aesthetic line with considerable exposure, but this last challenge can be bypassed on either side if you are so inclined. Heading left requires dropping into the top of Dead Dog Couloir and onto steep snow until midsummer, so have your ice ax out to avoid a rapid, unplanned descent (the climbers ascending the couloir wouldn't appreciate this). Bypassing the gray rock band to the right involves somewhat grungy climbing on gravel and slabs and can be quite exciting with a little new snow.

To climb the gray tower directly, start on a ledge on its right side. Traverse for a few feet with good handholds on the top of the blocks before regaining the ridge top and balancing along to its end.

Now 100 yards from the summit of Torreys, scramble up loose talus and join the hordes for lunch.

After lunch, descend on the trail to the saddle connecting Torreys with Grays Peak. From here you can either jog on over to Grays and descend the Grays Peak Trail shown on the topo map, or you can do a descending traverse on a reasonably well-defined trail to join the Grays Peak Trail at 13,600 feet. From here, follow the trail back to the trailhead.

Another option early in the season is to follow the descending traverse described above until you have access to one of two snow gullies that provide a fun and rapid descent into the bowl at the 12,640-foot level. Make sure that conditions are safe before committing to the snow. These slopes can avalanche. Rejoin the trail and follow it back to the trailhead.

The Gray Tower at the head of the Dead Dog Couloir is normally considered to be the crux of the route.

49. The Citadel to Pettingell Traverse

The Citadel to Pettingell Traverse forms the skyline in this view.

ROUND-TRIP DISTANCE	9.4 miles
ROUND-TRIP TIME	7 hours
STARTING ELEVATION	10,296 feet
HIGHEST ELEVATION	13,553 feet
ELEVATION GAIN	3,800 feet
SEASON	June through September
JURISDICTION	Arapaho National Forest, Clear Creek Ranger District
MAPS	Grays Peak 7.5 minute; Loveland Pass 7.5 minute

OVERVIEW: A pleasant trail and off-trail approach with difficult climbing on the ridge, requiring the use of a rope.

GETTING THERE: The Herman Gulch Trailhead is reached by taking exit 218 from Interstate 70, 2.8 miles west of the Bakerville exit. Park in the large

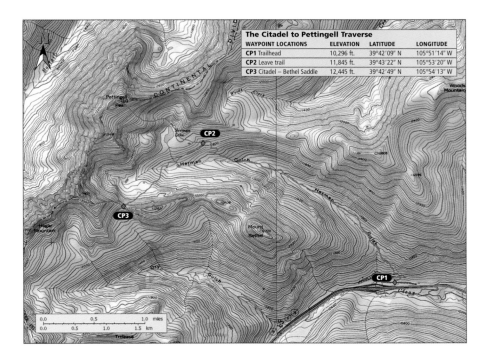

The Citadel to Pettingell Traverse			
WAYPOINT LOCATIONS	ELEVATION	LATITUDE	LONGITUDE
CP1 Trailhead	10,296 ft.	39°42'09" N	105°51'14" W
CP2 Leave trail	11,845 ft.	39°43'22" N	105°53'20" W
CP3 Citadel – Bethel Saddle	12,445 ft.	39°42'49" N	105°54'13" W

parking lot on the north side of the highway. (Note: There have been several break-ins to vehicles parked in this area. Take the usual precautions.)

COMMENT: The Citadel has long been a climbers' objective. With a spectacular location and several options for rock and snow routes (not to mention its proximity to the Denver metro area), this isn't surprising. However, when combined with a ridge traverse to Pettingell Peak, the quality of this scramble is dramatically enhanced.

APPROACH: From the parking area (CP1), take the popular Herman Gulch Trail for 2.9 miles to CP2, where you leave the trail.

ROUTE DESCRIPTION: From CP2, contour around the basin to the obvious saddle between the Citadel and Mount Bethel (CP3). A faint trail will help on the last 100 feet or so of the ascent to this saddle.

Walk west up the grassy ridge toward the summit block. Cliffs can be avoided on the left or can be climbed directly. When you reach the east end of the summit block, traverse right on loose ledges to a gully providing a reasonable route to the summit ridge (Class 4).

One of many short steps in the ridge over to Pettingell.

Note that most parties instead go to the left and ascend via a loose gully on the south side—definitely a less aesthetic route unless there is snow in the gully.

After reaching the south summit, the view over to the north summit is spectacular, but apart from a short Class 4 downclimb to the saddle, there are no real difficulties.

It is after reaching the north summit that the real challenges begin, with several difficult downclimbs along the ridge to Pettingell.

All but one step can be reasonably downclimbed. We were comfortable downclimbing unroped for all but 10 to 15 feet of the major step, at which point we broke out the rope.

The consensus is that this short pitch is about 5.4, so many parties would also want to rope up if reversing this route.

Randy planning his move above the crux downclimb/rappel.

After this, the difficulties are essentially over. The walk over to Pettingell Peak should be uneventful.

From the summit of Pettingell, there are several options for the descent to Herman Lake. The most direct descends southeast down scree slopes to the broad bench directly northwest of Herman Lake. Here you may pick up a trail that avoids a cliff band above the lake by heading generally east into a shallow, grassy gully. At the lake, regain the main trail and head down to the car.

Looking back at the crux.

A view from Pettingell Peak towards the Citadel, showing the connecting ridge. Old mountain goat in foreground.

50. Mount Bancroft—East Ridge

The east ridge of Mount Bancroft.

ROUND-TRIP DISTANCE	3.5 miles from the Loch Lomond parking area
ROUND-TRIP TIME	3.5 hours
STARTING ELEVATION	11,214 feet
HIGHEST ELEVATION	13,250 feet
ELEVATION GAIN	2,230 feet
SEASON	Year-round, though with snow on the route it is considerably more of a challenge
JURISDICTION	Arapaho National Forest, Clear Creek Ranger District
MAP	Empire, 7.5 minute

OVERVIEW: A short but very enjoyable scramble on solid rock. One rappel allows you to stay on the ridge crest the whole way. Lots of Class 3 and a few Class 4 moves.

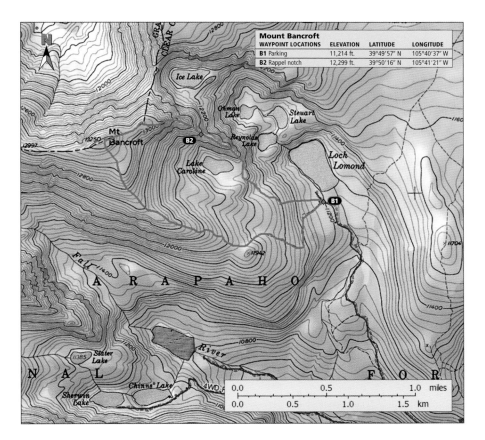

Mount Bancroft			
WAYPOINT LOCATIONS	ELEVATION	LATITUDE	LONGITUDE
B1 Parking	11,214 ft.	39°49'57" N	105°40'37" W
B2 Rappel notch	12,299 ft.	39°50'16" N	105°41'21" W

GETTING THERE: Take the Fall River Road exit from Interstate 70 (exit 238). Head north on this paved road for 8.3 miles. Turn left onto Alice Road, and after 1 mile, turn right onto Stewart Road (Forest Service Road 7012). Drive or hike up this rough four-wheel-drive road for 2.2 miles to a parking area by Loch Lomond.

COMMENT: The east ridge of Bancroft provides an excellent training ground for some of the more committing routes described in this guidebook.

This route has long been used by experienced alpinists in the winter and spring due to its relatively good access and moderate avalanche potential. More than one group has been forced back before ever reaching the base of the route by the savage winter winds that characterize this area.

The views can be very enjoyable. One morning when we climbed this ridge, the Front Range was languishing under a sea of clouds, providing the

Rappelling the notch.

PHOTO BY CHARLIE WINGER

Climbing out of the notch on the left side of the rock step keeps the difficulty to Class 4.

kind of views often seen on Mount Rainier. Most parties will require a full-length rope for one rappel, even in the summer conditions described here.

Stewart Road (Forest Service Road 7012) will probably be closed by snow-drifts at some point until at least mid-June, adding to the length of the trip. Two gates along this road, also known as the Loch Lomond Road, are closed during winter and spring months. Specifically the lower gate is closed from December 1–June 1, while the upper gate is closed from October 15–July 15.

APPROACH: From the parking area by the lake (B1), head west, picking your way through low-growing vegetation to the flat part of the ridge just east of Lake Caroline. From here, walk up the initially gentle slopes of the ridge.

ROUTE DESCRIPTION: Continue on easy terrain until you reach the obvious gap in the ridge.

This gap requires a 75-foot rappel for most parties, although difficult downclimbing on the climbers' left looks possible. (Note: Don't trust old slings found there. On one occasion, a sling reportedly left there a few weeks earlier had been completely chewed through by critters. Also, avoid sharp-edged rocks on the lip—these could easily cut a rope.)

Once you are down into the notch, look ahead at the route's crux. In the middle of the face is a crack system (concensus 5.2), but this can be avoided by going either right or left. Either way provides good climbing with one or two Class 4 moves.

Above the notch.

After this crux, the climbing becomes Class 2 and 3 scrambling on excellent rock. As the angle eases, head over the false summit on grassy slopes.

Descend via the gentle slopes of the southeast ridge. Pick up a jeep road not shown on the map and return to the parking area.

Class 3 scrambling on the upper ridge.

ABOUT THE AUTHOR

 Born in Yorkshire, England, Dave Cooper holds a doctorate in physics from the University of Durham. He has spent the last twenty-eight years exploring the Colorado Mountains and has climbed extensively in many of the world's great ranges, including the Andes, the Himalayas, the Canadian Rockies, and the Alaska Range. Dave is the author of *Colorado Snow Climbs: A Guide For All Seasons* and writes the "Trail Mix" column for *The Denver Post*.

Ginni and Laura enjoying the scrambling on Music Mountain.

INDEX